SPIRITUALLY
ANCHORED
IN UNSETTLED TIMES

OTHER BOOKS BY BRUCE C. HAFEN

The Broken Heart: Applying the Atonement to Life's Experiences
The Believing Heart: Nourishing the Seed of Faith
The Belonging Heart, with Marie K. Hafen
A Disciple's Life: The Biography of Neal A. Maxwell
Covenant Hearts: Marriage and the Joy of Human Love

SPIRITUALLY
ANCHORED
IN UNSETTLED TIMES

BRUCE C. HAFEN

DESERET
BOOK

SALT LAKE CITY, UTAH

Library of Congress Cataloging-in-Publication Data

Hafen, Bruce C.
    Spiritually anchored in unsettled times / Bruce C. Hafen.
        p. cm.
    Includes bibliographical references and index.
    ISBN 978-1-60641-069-1 (hardbound : alk. paper)
1. Christian life—Mormon authors. 2. Church of Jesus Christ of
Latter-day Saints—Doctrines. 3. Mormon Church—Doctrines. I. Title.
    BX8656.H33 2009
    248.4'89332—dc22   2008052629

Printed in the United States of America
Publishers Printing, Salt Lake City, UT

10   9   8   7   6   5   4   3   2   1

To our most important young investigators:

Sarah, Ben, Spencer, Joshua, Eliza, Samuel, and Hannah
Devin, Lauren, Abby, Michael, Anna, Claire, Lizzy, and Emma
Daniel, Chaya, Caleb, Elia, Asher, Micah, and Devorah
Lydia, Hannah, Emma, Clark, Kayla, Ellie, and Brigham
Holden, Ethan, Caleb, Eve, Peter, and Marie
Madison, Zachary, Jacob, and Joshua
and Cadence

Behold, they are . . . as a vessel . . . tossed about

upon the waves without sail or anchor, or without

anything wherewith to steer her.

MORMON 5:18

CONTENTS

ACKNOWLEDGMENTS

I thank Sheri Dew, Eric d'Evegnee, Amy Birk Hafen, Fran Clark Hafen, Marie Kartchner Hafen, Tom Hafen, Tracy Taylor Hafen, and Martha Johnson for reading an earlier version of this manuscript and for offering many worthwhile suggestions. I am also grateful to the publication and production team at Deseret Book—Cory Maxwell, Suzanne Brady, Shauna Gibby, Tonya-Rae Facemyer, and Rachael Ward—for their competence and their patient support.

I express appreciation to Brigham Young University for the opportunity to present much of the content of chapters 1 and 2 at a BYU devotional in February 2008; to the Neal A. Maxwell Institute for Religious Scholarship at BYU for the opportunity to present most of the content in chapters 7 and 8 at the second annual Neal A. Maxwell Lecture in March 2008; and to the Missionary Training Center in Provo, Utah, for the opportunity to present parts of chapters 3 and 4 at an MTC devotional in May 2008. Chapters 5 and 6 draw on a much earlier BYU devotional address. This book is a personal expression and not an official statement of Church doctrine.

INTRODUCTION

This book begins by discussing a disciple's journey, even though *Anchored* is the main word in the book's title. How can we go anywhere when we are anchored? That sounds like being held in place, unable to move. Is that any way to go on a journey? Yet the tension between being anchored and going forward is actually a productive gospel paradox, an apparent contradiction that resolves into greater meaning upon deeper inquiry.

Think of a mountain climber ascending steep, rocky cliffs. He needs anchor points planted firmly in the rocks, so he has sure places to tie his ropes and to put his feet. In that sense, being well anchored is crucial to his ability to keep moving upward.

So it is with a disciple's journey, which must often traverse rugged, high terrain and turbulent seas. The disciple needs to be fixed and secure in his relationship with the Lord in order to move ever closer to Him—especially against the stiff winds of opposition, which sometimes whistle loudest around the highest peaks.

As one friend said, we must increase the depth of our testimonies in order to decrease the distance between ourselves and the Savior. Or in the words of President Thomas S. Monson, "If we do not have a deep foundation of faith and a solid testimony of truth, we may have difficulty withstanding the harsh storms and icy winds of adversity which inevitably come to each of us."[1]

The prophet Ether understood how being anchored is essential to a stable spiritual journey: "Wherefore, whoso believeth in God might with surety hope for a better world, yea, even a place at the right hand of God, which hope cometh of faith, maketh an anchor to the souls of men, which would make them sure and steadfast, always abounding in good works, being led to glorify God" (Ether 12:4).

Against this background, Part I describes eight stages in a disciple's journey. These steps then provide a context for considering in later chapters some specific anchor points we need to ensure our continued momentum at any point along the journey—basic points of reference to resolve questions about testimony, uncertainty, and conflicts between faith and reason. These issues reflect the unsettled times in which we live, a context that provided much of the motivation for preparing these essays.

For example, I have noticed lately a number of people who are thrown off course by unexpected attacks on their testimony of the gospel. A neighbor recently dropped by with urgent concerns about a member of his family who without warning just announced that he had lost his faith—not only in the Restoration but in God. Not long ago a former missionary companion called seeking help for his grandson, a returned missionary who said that he no longer believed that God really answers prayers.

I have also noticed a tendency among some Church members, especially younger ones, to see testimony and inspiration as primarily a good feeling. Feelings are especially important when they come as an actual confirmation of other evidence of truth. That confirmation is essential to our spiritual guidance. But in addition to our feelings, a well-grounded testimony also includes other important elements, such as experience and reason. Feeling by itself has a thin root system that is too shallow to support a fully developed testimony, especially when confronting hard questions, adversity, or people who might try to manipulate our feelings. An overemphasis on feeling alone runs the risk of creating a fair-weather faith that is "all sail and no anchor."[2]

Another challenge that asks for deeper anchoring is that many of us, despite our good intentions, simply get stuck along the growth path of becoming true followers of Christ, and our personal spiritual development slows to a halt even though we remain active in the Church. In today's option-overdosed world, some can get stuck simply because of distractions—being diverted from a serious quest by any number of enticing but often trivial side canyons. Distractions can stop our serious progress as effectively as a conscious choice to quit moving. Some grind to a halt under the weight of overload and exhaustion. Others may begin to care more about being comfortable than about growing—

perhaps because growth is too often accompanied by growing pains and stretch marks.

We wouldn't lose momentum in these ways if more of us could live every day as truly consecrated disciples of Christ, rather than just being active in the Church. Those who are well-intentioned but stuck in mere activity wonder why the joy of the journey has waned, perhaps without realizing that they have stopped growing spiritually. When the growth stops, so does the joy.

The idea of being active but missing the joy echoes Aldous Huxley's phrase about those who want "Christianity without tears."[3] That kind of Christianity spares its adherents the tears of sorrow, but, by definition, it also removes the tears of true joy. That is a Garden of Eden kind of Christianity, where one remains "in a state of innocence [and undisturbed comfort], having no joy, for they knew no misery" (2 Nephi 2:23).

Whatever the reason for our lost momentum, it isn't enough to just go through the motions—we must be in motion. We can't move toward a sanctified state of faithfulness just by checking an attendance box, because our spiritual growth is a developmental process, not a yes-or-no event. The power to keep moving can and must originate in an internal motivation that is anchored enough in our own authentic testimony to reignite our motion again and again, overcoming the inertia that holds us back and returning us to our desired course. When we exert enough spiritual energy to move closer to the Savior, the good news is that He then moves closer to us, more than doubling our motion by joining it with His.

These three issues—testimony, uncertainty, and the distinction between being active and being truly consecrated—have a common core. A shallow testimony is often linked with being vulnerable to the risks of uncertainty, and those who experience both are more likely to assume that mere activity is the point of Church membership. They may not even be conscious of the distinction between being active and being consecrated.

No matter what tempest tosses us most upon life's seas, even when our "ship [is] covered with the waves," becoming more deeply anchored in the spiritual foundations of Christ's true followers will bless, energize, and change us as we journey toward the eternal presence of Him whom "even the winds and the sea obey" (Matthew 8:24, 27).

Part I

A DISCIPLE'S JOURNEY

Chapter 1

FROM DARKNESS TOWARD THE LIGHT

A few years ago our then-teenaged daughter was feeling quite unsettled, asking some very honest questions, such as, "Why is life so hard?" As Marie and I talked with her over dinner, I prayed as a missionary would for the right thing to say. After all, our children and grandchildren are our most important investigators.

In that moment, I received a prompting about gravitational pull. I grabbed a paper napkin and drew a sketch I'd never thought of before, which sparked a lively discussion. I felt very close to her that night. She is the child of our covenant, and I want to be with her always.

I'd like to share here the sketch from that napkin. Pretend that you and I are sitting in some cozy Italian restaurant, and I've been lucky enough to find a napkin with no tomato sauce on it. Let's call this sketch "A Disciple's Journey."

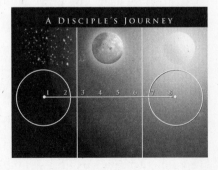

The illustration shows that a disciple moves from darkness into light, increasing from the dim light of the stars, to the moon, and then to the brightness of the sun (a more detailed, color version follows page 36). Joseph Smith compared these heavenly bodies with the telestial, terrestrial, and celestial kingdoms. As the temple teaches, we can and should move toward that celestial light during mortality. We do live in the world, but we need not be of the world.

Notice that two vertical lines separate the sun, moon, and stars. Each line suggests a major transition as we move from one stage to the next. However, the journey is not rigidly sequential. Over time, our experience may move us both forward and backward.

We see here two circles, each with a center point, in stage one and in stage three. These circles represent the gravitational pull from the opposing poles of our journey. In the darkness of stage one, the adversary, who claims to be the God of this world, exerts a constant force to hold us back from moving toward the light. As we cross the first barrier, we will leave the strongest satanic tugging, although he will always try to ensnare us wherever we are in the journey.

Reaching out from the center of light in stage three, Jesus also invites us with a spiritual gravitational pull toward Him. Think of the father of the prodigal son, praying his son home. When the father saw his son coming from afar, the father "had compassion, and ran" to his son "and fell on his neck, and kissed him" (Luke 15:20).

I compare that father to Christ, who is so eager for our return that He comes to meet us and strengthens us all along our way. Nephi wrote, "It is by grace that we are saved, after all we can do" (2 Nephi 25:23). Christ's running to us is a vivid symbol of that grace. We talk often in the Church about coming to Christ. Perhaps we should talk more about how Christ also comes to us.

No matter where we are on that path, we are never lost to Him. Sometimes we sing, "Who's on the Lord's side? Who?"[1] Let us also sing, "Be still, my soul: The Lord is on *thy side*."[2] We never have more value in the Lord's sight than when we are feeling worthless—as the prodigal son probably felt.

Various terms describe the overall process shown here. Mormon called disciples "true followers" of Christ—following the Son to return to the Father (Moroni 7:48). Moroni said, "Come unto Christ, and be perfected in him" (Moroni 10:32). Jesus asked, "What manner of men ought ye to be? . . . even as I am" (3 Nephi 27:27). Our Primary children sing, "I'm trying to be like Jesus."[3] Whatever we call it, this journey is the gospel's central concern.

Some non–Latter-day Saint observers of our Church think we haven't clearly taught this concept. One of them, Jan Shipps, said that while Mormons "emphasize . . . Christ's dying for humanity," they don't go on and "link the atonement to that part of the [LDS] 'plan of salvation' that involves progression toward godhood."[4] In other words, she thinks we haven't explained what the Atonement has to do with becoming like Jesus.

Another observer recently chided our Church for not explaining in a public way what he called our "doctrine of the perfectibility of mankind into divine form."[5] In fact, however, the Restoration answers these questions with stunning clarity. Consider the following steps as a direct response to such questions.

1. *Initiation*. As an act of will, we must take the first step that begins our journey. Some people take that initiative through their own desire to find and follow God. Think of Nephi, a believer who wanted to see what his father saw (1 Nephi 11:1–3). Think of Abraham, who desired "to be a greater follower of righteousness" (Abraham 1:2).

Some who live worldly lives finally decide they've had enough of Satan's darkness, like the prodigal son when "he came to himself" and headed for home (Luke 15:17). Some, like Enos or young Alma, start moving when they remember the teachings of their parents (Enos 1:3–4; Alma 36:17–18). Many others initiate their journey when they accept the invitation of a missionary or another Church member to listen to the message of the Restoration.

Often the Lord gives us a nudge by calling us, perhaps to serve a mission, inviting us to become, like Mormon, "a disciple of Jesus Christ" who is "called of him to declare his word among his people" (3 Nephi 5:13). Mormon referred to his own Church calling as a "gift" (Moroni 7:2), probably because he discovered that his calling gave him experiences that led him to truly come to know Christ. However we get started, the choice to begin this journey requires that we exert our will or at least desire to believe (Alma 32:27). God Himself cannot and will not force us to take that first step.

2. *Opposition*. But as soon as we start moving toward the light, the

gravitational pull of darkness will immediately try to jerk us back, for Satan "desireth to have you" (3 Nephi 18:18). He will tempt, frighten, and fight us.

Missionaries know all about this. One way or another, opposition will confront virtually every investigator. The first time Adam and Eve taught their children the gospel, Satan came along, saying, Don't believe your parents. So the children "believed it not, and they loved Satan more than God. And men began from that time forth to be carnal, sensual, and devilish" (Moses 5:13). "From that time forth" tells us that the children of Adam and Eve *chose* to be devilish *after* the Fall; they were not born devilish.

Satanic opposition has great power in today's world. Satan holds "a great chain in his hand" (Moses 7:26), which symbolizes such addictions as drugs, alcohol, and pornography. The prince of darkness looks up and laughs at the poor souls he ensnares.

But that opposition cannot destroy us. Remember Joseph praying in the grove—an enemy power bound his tongue "so that [he] could not speak" (Joseph Smith–History 1:15). Remember Moses when he first saw his grand vision. Satan came tempting him until Moses feared exceedingly, seeing the "bitterness of hell" (Moses 1:20). But both Joseph and Moses called upon God, who gave them power to drive Satan away (Joseph Smith–History 1:16; Moses 1:21). That is a key insight. Satan may rattle us, but he cannot overcome us, for God can and will cast Satan from our presence.

Lehi said, "It must needs be, that there is an opposition in all things" (2 Nephi 2:11). So wherever we are on our journey, there will always be a reason not to go on. We must not wait until all obstacles disappear. The purely rational mind will always find a good reason to hold back, for Satan places those reasons in our path. But opposition can strengthen us; it need not stop us. The skills of human growth are best learned "slowly, and against great difficulty."[6]

3. *First sacrifice.* When an investigator breaks free from the world's gravitational pull enough to repent and make serious covenants with God, he is ready for baptism—the clearest symbol of the first barrier of sacrifice. The first vertical line represents that barrier. This sacrifice requires, at a minimum, giving up the most obvious sins. As King Lamoni's father said, "I will give away all my sins to know thee" (Alma 22:18). By giving up short-term pleasures, he became free to seek far more lasting satisfactions.

This sacrifice asks us to live the most basic temporal commandments, such as tithing and the Word of Wisdom, which is "adapted to the capacity of . . . the weakest of [those who] can be called saints" (D&C 89:3). Often these are physical temptations. In the Judean wilderness, Satan first taunted the hungering Christ to change stones into bread and eat (Matthew 4:3).

For Church members who want to become serious disciples, the sacrament represents this first level of sacrifice. They also commit not only to give away their sins but also to remember Him and to follow Him until they know Him.

These early sacrifices do fix our feet on a disciple's path. For example, when Elder Neal A. Maxwell was an eighteen-year-old infantryman fighting on the island of Okinawa, he faced the most frightening night of his life. As enemy mortar shells exploded ever closer to his foxhole, he knelt in the mud and pledged his life to the Lord, if only he could be spared.

God answered his prayer with divine protection. But soon afterward, days of hot, rainy weather turned Okinawa into a giant swamp. Because the supply trucks bogged down in the mud, the support troops had such a hard time carrying food and water that the soldiers became unbearably thirsty. One historian said the only thing that saved them from their thirst was coffee, boiled and hand carried from distant supply points. Neal wrote his parents a card, saying he was keeping all the commandments, but "the coffee is tempting at times." Yet despite the constant thirst, he refused to drink the coffee. He did find a way to get just a little water. He said he caught rain water in his helmet to bless his sacrament each week.[7] Young Neal knew that God had heard him, and he showed his gratitude by sacrifice. His disciple's journey gained traction in the mud of Okinawa.

As a young missionary, Elder Gordon B. Hinckley found himself in a foxhole of a different sort. From the spiritual trenches of England, he became so discouraged that he told his father he might as well return home. His father wrote back, "Dear Gordon, . . . forget yourself and go to work." Stung by that counsel, Gordon threw himself into the work.[8] After two years of his working and forgetting himself, his mission president sent him to tell the First Presidency why they needed better missionary materials. That visit to Church headquarters was supposed to last fifteen minutes but ended up lasting more than seventy years. President Hinckley's entire life was about forgetting himself and going to work. His constant willingness to sacrifice kept his feet moving on a disciple's path.

4. *Forgiveness and the Holy Ghost.* Repentance and forgiveness eliminate the rubbish and the bad habits that can hold us captive in the worldly orbit. But we can receive the Holy Ghost as a constant companion only *after* being cleansed by water. Christ told the Nephites to "be baptized in my name, [so] that ye may be sanctified by the reception of the Holy Ghost" (3 Nephi 27:20). Receiving the Holy Ghost is the baptism by fire. Because that fire purges and purifies, it truly launches the refining process of becoming like Jesus—meaning, to become saintly, or sanctified.

Let's clarify a point here that we sometimes miss. Some describe the entire process of spiritual growth in terms limited to faith, repentance, baptism, and the Holy Ghost, as if once we've received the gift of the Holy Ghost, the hard work is done and our exaltation is assured—so long as we don't do something seriously wrong. Endure to the end, we say, as if that means relaxing in some eternal rocking chair. God will just reel us in, like a fish on a line. But it's not quite that simple.

On the contrary, receiving the Holy Ghost marks the *beginning* of our real spiritual growth, not the *end* of it. Baptism and the Holy Ghost only let us "[enter] in by the gate" (2 Nephi 31:18; emphasis added).

Then the Holy Ghost leads us along the "strait and narrow path" of becoming sanctified disciples—not as passive spectators but by our straining every spiritual muscle, drinking in the power of temple ordinances, overcoming adversity, and feasting actively on Christ's words to nourish us in becoming ever more holy (2 Nephi 31:19; 32:3). And the long-term goal of that journey is to become like Him.

Does the Atonement have anything to do with this higher, developmental part of the journey, or is it limited to the forgiveness part? Moroni taught that Christ's grace helps move us well beyond forgiveness toward becoming like Him, or sanctified: "Come unto Christ, and be perfected in him, . . . then are ye sanctified in Christ by the grace of God" (Moroni 10:32–33).

One Australian convert wrote to her mother, who couldn't understand why the daughter had joined the Church: "My past life [was a] wilderness of weeds, with hardly a flower strewed among them. Now how different, the weeds have vanished, and flowers spring up in their place."[9]

The Atonement helps us grow in two ways: removing negative weeds and cultivating positive flowers. The Savior's grace blesses both parts—if we do our part. First and repeatedly we must uproot the weeds of sins and bad habits. It isn't enough just to *mow* them. Rather, we must yank them out by the roots through real repentance. But forgiveness only begins our growth. We are not just paying a debt; we want and need to become like Him. So once we've cleared our heart-land, we must continually plant and nourish new seeds of divine qualities.

Then as our self-discipline and His gifts come together, "the flow'rs of grace appear," such as hope and meekness.[10] The very tree of life will also grow in this garden of the heart, bearing fruit so sweet that it lifts all our burdens "through the joy of his Son" (Alma 33:23). And when the flower of charity blooms here, we will love others with Christlike compassion.

We all need grace, both to overcome sinful weeds and to grow divine flowers in ways we cannot fully do alone. But grace is not cheap. It is very expensive, even dear. How much does this grace cost? Is it enough just to believe in Christ? Like King Lamoni's father, the man who found the pearl of great price gave "all that he had" for it (Matthew 13:46; see also Alma 22:15). The Savior asks *all that we have* if we would seek "all that my Father hath" (D&C 84:38.)

To qualify for such treasure, our sacrifice must somehow emulate Christ's own sacrifice, of which He said: "How exquisite you know not, yea, how hard to bear you know not" (D&C 19:15). No wonder Paul said we are "joint-heirs with Christ; *if so be that we suffer with him*" (Romans 8:17; emphasis added). All of His heart, all of our hearts.

What pearl could possibly be worth such a price for us and for Him? This earth is not our home. We are away at school, doing hard home-work, learning from opposition how to grow up, spiritually, so we can return Home. Yet this is "the great plan of happiness" (Alma 42:8). Over and over the Lord tells us why the plan is worth our sacrifice—and His: "The joy of our redemption" (Moses 5:11). "That I may receive this great joy" (Alma 22:15). "That happiness which is prepared for the saints" (2 Nephi 9:43). Afflictions, yes—His and ours—because so much is at stake. But like molten gold in the ashes of affliction, we will also find "incomprehensible joy" (Alma 28:8).

Christ's Atonement is at the very core of this plan. Without His sacrifice, there would be no way Home, no way to be together, no way to be like Him. He gave us all He had. Why? Because "how great is *his* joy" (D&C 18:13; emphasis added) when even one of us "gets it"— when we look up from the weed patch and head for Home, even if at first we barely stumble forward.

Only the restored gospel has the fullness of these truths. Yet the evil one is engaged in one of history's greatest cover-ups, trying to persuade people that this Church knows least—when in fact it knows most—about how our relationship with Christ makes true Christians of us.

To summarize, after helping us weed out our worldly ways with the balm of forgiveness, Christ's perfecting grace then helps us replace those weeds with the divine flowers of Christlike attributes. You might say He wants to plant a divine garden in us. But we must satisfy certain conditions for this growth to occur, just as we had to satisfy the condition of repentance in order to receive forgiveness. The next steps in our journey illustrate some of those other conditions.

5. *An eye single to God's glory.* Describing a disciple's journey from darkness into light, the Lord told the early Saints: "And if your eye be single to my glory, your whole bodies shall be filled with light, and

there shall be no darkness in you; and that body which is filled with light comprehendeth all things" (D&C 88:67).

Having an eye single to God is, then, just one condition we *must satisfy* before the Atonement can bless us with the attributes of divinity. As Moroni said, "Touch not . . . the unclean thing" and "deny yourselves of all ungodliness," "then are ye sanctified" (Moroni 10:30, 32, 33).

But that is hard to do, because our culture today is saturated with being double-minded and indulging in unclean things. One of the principal themes of the Book of Mormon describes the recurring cycle of pride and sin. Groups among Lehi's posterity often moved from prosperity to transgression and apostasy and then they returned in humility and sorrowful repentance to God. I once heard President Hinckley mention this familiar cycle with a new insight. He said that prosperity often leads to *indulgence,* and indulgence leads to sin. Said another way, indulgence is the bridge that leads us from prosperity to sin.

Prosperous but believing people are less likely to be tempted by outright sin; yet the adversary can much more easily seduce them with the allure of indulging themselves—at first, just a little; but by then they're on the bridge that leads them carefully away.

Indulgence means gratifying our vain desires in the proud belief that we deserve to have it all, keeping one hand on the wall of the temple and one foot on the dance floor at Club Babylon. Every day we hear messages of indulgence from today's culture of self-absorption and personal entitlement: you are entitled a life of pleasure; go ahead, pamper yourself—you deserve it. I saw a billboard recently in Utah: "Modesty has never been sexier." Talk about double-mindedness. We live in a society that, increasingly, seems to have no higher aim than satisfying its own indulgent whims.

Many people in our liberated culture feel they have a right to indulge themselves by eating too much, spending too much, and reveling in creature comforts. But, as one friend said, If you don't get out of your comfort zone, you won't learn. And, we might add, If you don't learn, you won't grow. And if you don't grow, you won't find joy. To be denied true joy is a high price to pay for indulging in self-satisfied comfort. One Christmas song speaks of "comfort and joy" as if they always go together.[11] But if we want comfort too much, we won't find joy.

Today's flood of pornography often results from overindulgence, and it deprives those who choose it from knowing true joy. Alma told his son to "bridle all your passions." Why? So "that you may be filled with love" (Alma 38:12). Pornography addictions can destroy marriages, shattering the authentic romantic dream of eternal love. Think of the irony: Fake love can destroy real love. What a cheap and dirty trick!

And worse, yielding to pornography in the first place is a classic example of touching the unclean thing, of refusing to deny oneself of ungodliness. This double-mindedness has consequences: we cannot then be perfected in Christ—not because he lacks the power but because we lack the discipline. Thank heaven that repentance, as demanding as that can be with addictive behavior, can restore discipline.

Chapter 2

"WITH YOU"—IN THE LIGHT
OF HIS LOVE

As we approach the next vertical line in our diagram—the second barrier of sacrifice—we move symbolically from the moon to the sun. All of the moon's light is reflected from the sun; it is borrowed light. When life's greatest tests come, those who are living on the borrowed testimonies of others will not be able to stand. We need our own access to the light of the Son.

6. *Second sacrifice*. Baptism represents the first sacrifice. The temple endowment represents the second sacrifice. The first sacrifice was about breaking out of Satan's orbit. The second sacrifice is about breaking fully into Christ's orbit, enticed and welcomed by His gravitational pull. The first sacrifice was about giving up mostly temporal things. The second one is about consecrating ourselves spiritually, holding back nothing. Elder Neal A. Maxwell said that the only thing we can give the Lord that He hasn't already given us is our own will.[1]

Wanting to be meek and lowly, faithful disciples gladly offer God their will. In the words our children sing,

> *I feel my Savior's love*
>
> . . . .
>
> *He knows I will follow Him,*
> *Give all my life to Him.*"[2]

And then what happens? In President Ezra Taft Benson's words, "When obedience ceases to be an irritant and becomes our quest, in that moment God will endow us with power."[3]

Not long before he passed away, I heard Elder Neal A. Maxwell say, "It would change the entire Church if in every ward, we could have just three or four more families who became truly consecrated disciples of Jesus Christ instead of just being active in the Church."[4]

Three brief stories illustrate the sacrificial difference between just being active and being truly consecrated. In 1936, my father served in the presidency of the St. George, Utah, stake, which then included part of northwestern Arizona. One day he wrote in his journal that their stake presidency had a problem with several members of the high council. These brethren would grumble and make excuses when they were assigned to drive sixty miles on a Sunday to visit the Saints in Mt. Trumbull, Arizona, on monthly stake speaking assignments. Nobody liked to go to Mt. Trumbull because the rough gravel road was tough on their cars and the branch was so far from St. George. When one high councilor complained that the stake presidency always assigned him to go, they checked their records and found that he had been to Mt. Trumbull only once in the past three years. Another high councilor had to be assigned four months in a row before, as my father wrote, "Mt. Trumbull was finally honored with his presence."

My father contrasted these men with one of their youngest high councilors, who was always "willing to perform faithfully every call we have made on him, including buying his own gas." Then he wrote, "I'm just wondering, is a man really converted if he isn't willing to sacrifice for his religion; and if he isn't converted, [should he be a Church leader]? Can there be degrees of conversion?"[5]

Now compare that experience with another Arizona story. In the late 1800s, the Church began sending settlers from Utah to Arizona. But Arizona was a desolate place, and some of those families had a very rough time. One settler in the Gila Valley said of the local plants and animals, "If you touch it, it stings you; if you pet it, it bites you; and if you eat it, it kills you." In 1854, United States general William T. Sherman said, "We had one war with Mexico and took Arizona. We should have another and compel them to take it back."[6]

In 1898, Andrew Kimball, age forty, had a nice home and a young family in Salt Lake City, including a three-year-old son named Spencer. The First Presidency called Andrew to be the stake president in Arizona's Gila Valley, to serve for what turned out to be the rest of his life—twenty-six years. Moving to the deserts of Arizona in those days was so difficult that, as Andrew wrote in his journal, he and his wife, Olive, "bowed before God trying to pray while their hearts were so swollen with grief. They bubbled over with scalding tears."[7] The quickest route from Salt Lake City to Thatcher, their new home, was two thousand miles by train through California or Colorado. His friends thought being sent to Arizona was like being buried alive. But Andrew wrote in his journal that he "had been called on a mission and to me there was but one answer and that was to go."[8]

As an Arizona boy, young Spencer Kimball watched his parents repeatedly take their problems to the Lord. They always had family prayer. They frequently fasted. They always paid their tithing. When Spencer was old enough to gather eggs from their chickens, his mother taught him to put aside one egg in every ten to pay their tithing. Once he walked with his mother to the bishop's house to take him what she called "the tithing eggs." Little Spencer asked her, "Are tithing eggs different than other eggs?" She said the tithing eggs belonged to Heavenly Father. From then on, gathering eggs had new meaning for Spencer.[9]

He also remembered hearing his father say at haying time, "The best hay is on the west side of the field. Get your load for the tithing barn from that side. And load it full and high."[10] The Kimballs gave Heavenly Father the very best they had. As a result, Heavenly Father gave them the very best He had. Many years later, the whole Church learned how growing up in the adversities of Arizona had prepared Spencer W. Kimball to be a tower of spiritual strength as the Lord's living prophet.

Reflecting this same pattern, Brigham Young called William and Elizabeth Wood in 1867 to help settle along the Muddy River in southern Nevada. One historian wrote that this colony faced more formidable challenges than had any western settlers.[11] To accept the call, the Woods sold their profitable butcher shop and their comfortable home in Salt Lake City.

Conditions in the Muddy settlement were so demanding that the colonists lived in severe poverty. As one descendant of the colonists later put it, "Those people were so poor, they couldn't even pay attention."[12] After five years of backbreaking effort, William's family lost everything when the settlement failed in 1872. The Woods returned penniless and exhausted to Salt Lake, where they lived in a dugout with a dirt floor and a sod roof.

One day William and Elizabeth stood looking at the beautiful home they had sold a few years earlier to accept their mission call. William asked her if she would like to have her house back. Elizabeth replied, "I would rather [live in a] dug-out with [our] mission filled, than [live] in that fine house with [our] mission unfulfilled."[13]

Why would Elizabeth Wood feel that way? Her answer says not simply that she was glad she had survived the hardships but that she honestly believed she was a different and better person because of the way she and her husband had faced the hardships together. She discovered an important secret about life that is known only to those who give all of their hearts to the Lord.

So what is the difference between people like the Kimballs or the Woods and those high councilors who didn't want to make the difficult sixty-mile drive from St. George to Mt. Trumbull? I believe my father was on to something important when he wrote, "Is a man really

converted if he isn't willing to sacrifice for his religion? . . . Can there
be degrees of conversion?"

We talk often about the distinction between being active in the
Church and being inactive. We should perhaps also talk more about
the additional difference between being active and being a truly consecrated disciple.

Choosing a life of consecration will of course take us out of our
comfort zone, just as it did the Kimballs and the Woods. But if we don't
leave our comfort zone, we won't stretch our way through all the steps
that eventually lead to true joy.

The Lord Himself described the meaning of being truly consecrated: "All among them who know their hearts are honest, and are
broken, and their spirits contrite, and are willing to observe their
covenants by sacrifice—yea, every sacrifice which I, the Lord, shall
command—they are accepted of me. For I, the Lord, will cause them
to bring forth as a very fruitful tree which is planted in a goodly land,
by a pure stream, that yieldeth much precious fruit" (D&C 97:8–9).

Those words describe what the Kimballs and the Woods became
through their consecration. They had broken hearts and contrite spirits. They were willing to make every sacrifice the Lord asked of them.
As a result, the Lord accepted them, and their lives bore much precious
fruit.

There is no greater source of inner peace than to know that our
lives are acceptable to the Lord. Where does that sense of acceptance
come from? In the sixth lecture on faith, Joseph Smith taught: "It is

through the medium of the sacrifice of all earthly things that men do actually know that they are doing the things that are well pleasing in the sight of God." He added that those who are unwilling to accept this spirit of total sacrifice do not know that the course of their lives is acceptable to God. They remain in a state of doubt and uncertainty, which makes them unable "to contend against all the opposition, tribulations, and afflictions which they will have to encounter in order to be . . . joint heirs with Christ Jesus; and they will grow weary in their minds, and the adversary will have power over them and destroy them."[14]

7. *Divine tutorial.* As we feel the power of Christ's love pulling us toward Him, we anticipate the joy of His promise: "Be faithful and diligent . . . , and I will encircle thee in the arms of my love" (D&C 6:20).

The Lord reflected that affection in the way He addressed Joseph Smith. During Joseph's early years, Christ called him "my *servant* Joseph" (for example, D&C 1:17; emphasis added). But after Joseph had traveled long paths marked by consecration and hardship, the Lord said, "From henceforth I shall call you *friends*" (D&C 84:77; emphasis added).

What is the difference between a servant and a friend? The Lord had earlier said, "The *servant* knoweth not what his lord doeth: but I have called you *friends*; for all things that I have heard of my Father I have made known unto you" (John 15:15; emphasis added).

The Lord's "friends" thus feel His increased confidence in them—enough confidence that He is now willing to tutor them in the most personal ways. But they also discover that His tutorial asks more of them, not less. It is both possible and likely that the closer we come to Christ, the more we will be aware of what we yet need to do. He said, "*If* men come unto me I will show unto them their weakness. . . . if they humble themselves before me, . . . then will I make weak things become strong unto them" (Ether 12:27; emphasis added).

So if we are becoming more aware of our weaknesses, that doesn't mean we are drifting away from Him; it may well mean that we are drawing closer. Like a good coach, a good tutor will always help his students see and correct their mistakes. When we understand that, correction is motivating, not discouraging. For because of the Atonement, we can learn from our mistakes without being condemned by them.

The paradox of this divine tutorial is that the Lord will not only correct us but may also lead us into some forms of personal affliction. Because Elder Maxwell was such a faithful student of discipleship, I draw again from his words: "If we are serious about our discipleship, Jesus will eventually request each of us to do those very things which are the most difficult for us to do."[15] Thus, "sometimes the best people have the worst experiences because they are the most ready to learn."[16]

After Elder Maxwell learned he had the leukemia that eventually took his life, he shook his head and said he should have seen it coming. Why? Because ever since Okinawa, he had wanted to become a fully consecrated follower of Jesus, no matter what the price. And the more he desired the gift of charity—to love as Christ loves—the more he sensed how dear the price might be.

Christ's love is so deep that He took upon Himself the sins and afflictions of all mankind. Only in that way could He both pay for our sins and empathize with us enough to truly succor us—that is, run to us—with so much empathy that we can have complete confidence that He fully understands our sorrows. So, to love as Christ loves probably means we will taste some form of suffering ourselves, because the love and the affliction are but two sides of the same coin. Only by experiencing both sides to some degree can we begin to understand and love other people with a depth that even begins to approach Christ's love.

8. *Sanctification*. Sanctification is the stage when, finally, we are not only with God but *like* God, for only those who have become like Him can be with Him. As Jesus said, "It is enough for the disciple that he *be* as his master" (Matthew 10:25; emphasis added). This state of being is the hope, the vision, and the heart of a disciple's journey. Our deepest desire is, in the words of both John and Mormon, that "when he shall appear, we shall be like him" (1 John 3:2; Moroni 7:48).

Being like Him means we will possess His divine attributes, such as charity—loving others as He does. Do we develop charity by our own power, or is it a gift from God? Or is it both? Clearly we must be fully invested in Him, for He is fully invested in us. Only then will God "bestow" charity "upon all who are true followers of his Son" (Moroni 7:48). We can't develop a permanent Christlike love by ourselves, but we *can* do all in our power to become a "true follower"—meek, lowly of heart, and submissive to correction and affliction. Having charity thus requires both our total effort and His gift. When we have met the scriptural conditions, then the Comforter, the Holy Ghost, "filleth [us] with hope and perfect love, which love endureth . . . , until the end shall come, when all the saints [the sanctified] shall dwell with God" (Moroni 8:26).

On that day, we will no longer be God's servants or even His friends but something more. In Liberty Jail, Joseph Smith suffered so much that he learned both the affliction dimension and the charity dimension of Christ's love for him and for the Saints. Then Joseph was not just the Lord's servant or even His friend. Rather, God said, "My *son*, peace be unto thy soul; thine adversity and thine afflictions shall be but a small moment" (D&C 121:7; emphasis added).

Christ also invites each of us to grow from servant, to friend, to God's son or daughter. Then are we joint heirs with Christ. Then will we receive all that the Father hath—and all that the Father is:

"The Spirit itself beareth witness with our spirit, that we are the children of God: and if children, then heirs; heirs of God, and joint-heirs with Christ; if so be that we suffer with him, that we may be also glorified together. For I reckon that the sufferings of this present time are not worthy to be compared with the glory which shall be revealed in us" (Romans 8:16–18).

Earlier I mentioned our daughter. I said I want to be "with her" always. For me, the words "with you" capture the meaning of sanctification and the Atonement in their simplest terms. If we do our part, Christ makes us "at one" *with* God and *like* God, overcoming whatever separates us from Him. He is with us, *with you*, not only at the end of our lives but through each day of our lives. And without Christ, we could not be with our family and friends.

I first learned about "with you" in an unexpected way. A couple of years ago, Marie and I were in Sweden for the first international "Especially for Youth" (EFY) conference. As the concluding fireside began, the session director asked if we would say a few words to the youth about the Atonement. In earlier years, most youth leaders would have considered that topic too serious and abstract to interest many teenagers. But we knew from having been with them a few days that this group would take that subject seriously. Still, what do you say on this sacred theme, briefly and in untranslated English, that connects with Scandinavian teens, right where they live?

As we looked at those hundreds of bright-eyed young men and women, many of them the only Church member in their schools, I thought of how much it meant for them to be together. I had asked some of them that day how often they thought we should have EFY in their countries. One girl said, "I've never felt so good, just being with other good kids and having the Lord's Spirit with us. I think we should do this . . . every . . . *day*."

I saw on the walls some of the EFY banners with the assigned "group names" of youth teams who had been together all week. All the names used scriptural words, like "brightness," "dreamed a dream," "highly favored," and "happy still." I whispered to Marie what was for me a new idea. "You and I are a group, aren't we? Should we have a group name?" Her eyes lit up. "How about . . . 'with you?'" We agreed.

I told those young people that Marie's and my two-person group name—"with you"—meant we loved being with them and the two of us loved being with each other. And we knew they loved being together, drawing strength from faithful friends to take back home and steady them to stand, often alone, against the stiff winds of a worldly culture. Many devoted Young Single Adult counselors had been "with" the youth in their groups constantly in an unforgettable, week-long gospel conversation.

Then I told them that the Atonement simply means "with you," in two senses. First, it overcomes anything that separates us from our Heavenly Father, so we can be *with* Him; and Christ's Spirit can be with us—each day and forever. If we are faithful, some day, as He gathers us in, we will say, "O my Father, my Father, I am *with you* again."

Second, only through the Atonement can we be *with* our family members and friends forever. Once our daughter Emily had to run an errand, leaving her two-year-old son, Clark, with a babysitter. As she left, little Clark ran to her and cried longingly, "*With* you, Mom. *With* you." No longing is deeper than a toddler's desire to be with his mom—or than our hunger to be with those we love. The Atonement forever fulfills those longings.

Afterward I realized that I had used those words without checking to be sure that "with you" is a scriptural phrase (which an EFY group name should be), though I just knew it would be in the scriptures some place. The sacrament prayer says "with them," and Elijah told the young man, "They that be with us are more than they that be with them" (2 Kings 6:16). A computer search then led me to the exact words in a memorable context. In introducing the sacrament to the Nephites, Christ said, "And if ye do always remember me ye shall have my Spirit to be *with you*" (3 Nephi 18:11; emphasis added). So Christ first spoke the sacrament prayer as He personally taught what the sacrament is. And the promised "with you" is more than a formal prayer; it is His voice, speaking His promise of constant companionship to each of us.

"With you" also echoes Harriet Beecher Stowe's haunting lines from "Still, Still with Thee," which anticipates our return to God's presence:

> *But sweeter still to wake and find Thee there.*
> *So shall it be at last, in that bright morning*
> *When the soul waketh and life's shadows flee;*
> *Oh, in that hour, fairer than daylight dawning,*
> *Shall rise the glorious thought, I am with Thee!*[17]

Still *with* Thee. *Still*—always; and *still*—quiet.

Like still water, the doctrine of Christ's peace runs deep, and it deserves to be held in the most reverent space in our hearts. And for me, "still, still with Thee" means being not only with Jesus but also with Marie, with our family, always. My heart has no greater desire. On that day of celestial reunion we will fully comprehend what it means to be there, together, something we would never understand without having endured our long, hard journey in the earth school. I believe we will gasp as we realize we are actually there, in that place, sensing "the glorious thought, I am *with Thee!*"

Jesus is the Christ, the great Uniter, the Atoning One. Because of what He did, we too can be with Him; with our dearest ones, still, always, to "go no more out" (Revelation 3:12). Then the disciple's journey is complete. Then the disciple will be like—and be with—his Master.

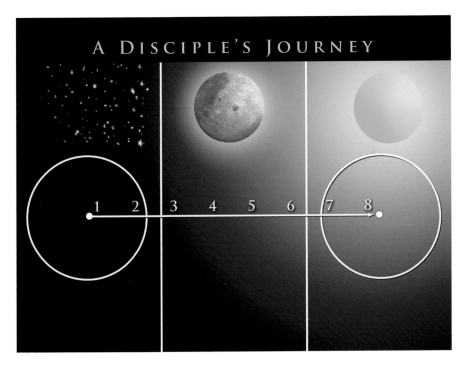

A DISCIPLE'S JOURNEY

1. Initiation

2. Opposition

3. First sacrifice

4. Forgiveness and the Holy Ghost

5. An eye single to God's glory

6. Second sacrifice

7. Divine tutorial

8. Sanctification

Part II

TESTIMONY

Chapter 3

HOW DO I KNOW?

While I was on a mission tour recently, the mission president told me that one of his missionaries had disappeared from his apartment that morning. After an anxious day, we learned that the missionary had just called his parents from a local airport to tell them he was coming home. When we received this news, we happened to be five minutes from that same airport. So the president and I walked into the airport to find a very surprised missionary standing near the pay phones. He embraced his president and tearfully apologized to him. We sat down to talk.

His main problem, he said, was that he didn't "feel" he had a testimony. He said, "I know I'm supposed to get a certain strong feeling after I pray. But I've been out here for six weeks. I've prayed and prayed, and the feeling just won't come." I wondered where he had gained the impression that a testimony is only a feeling. That evening we tried to help him be more patient and to understand more fully what a testimony is and how it develops.

Of course spiritual confirmation is crucial. It is ultimately the foundation of a genuine testimony. As the Apostle Paul wrote, "My speech and my preaching was not with enticing words of man's wisdom, but in demonstration of the Spirit and of power: that your faith should not stand in the wisdom of men, but in the power of God. [For] the natural man receiveth not the things of the Spirit of God: for they are foolishness unto him: neither can he know them, because they are spiritually discerned" (1 Corinthians 2:4–5, 14).

At the same time, it is possible to overemphasize feelings while neglecting other factors that add reinforcement to those feelings and protect against misinterpreting them.

For example, I know an experienced Church member who insisted that his point of view was inspired, even though his conclusion was directly at odds with existing Church policy and with the counsel of his priesthood leaders. He said he had prayed, and he had the feeling that his view was right. Therefore, he concluded, no one should question his feelings.

Our feelings are especially important when they come as a confirmation of other evidence of truth. But feeling alone can be too thin a reed to support a fully developed testimony. For that reason, we need to consider how feelings, anchored and tethered by other important sources of knowledge, fit into the overall process of gaining and keeping a testimony. We begin with a perspective on how missionaries teach investigators to gain a testimony, but we'll soon see that this pattern is a prototype for understanding how testimony grows in other contexts.

Missionaries need to understand what a testimony is and how it develops—first for their own spiritual security and then so they can teach their investigators how to recognize when God is manifesting the truth to them (see Moroni 10:4–5). Everything else a missionary teaches is secondary to the investigator's need for that testimony.

Testimony is also at the core of what parents and leaders all over the Church are trying to teach their children and youth. If those of the rising generation don't develop that internal assurance of truth, no amount of other information or activity we give them will matter very much.

The goal of the first lesson in *Preach My Gospel* is to help investigators begin the process of discovering their own testimony. Imagine a triangle showing "God" at the top and "missionaries" and investigator" in the corners below.

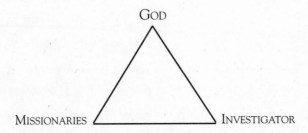

The lines connecting the triangle's three corners establish three key relationships: one, between God and the missionaries; two, between the missionaries and the investigator; and three, between the investigator and God.

At the base of the triangle, the horizontal relationship between the missionaries and the investigator is crucial. Here the missionaries teach, listen to, and love the investigator. But the missionary-investigator relationship, as important as it is, is not the ultimate key to testimony and conversion. The real key lies in the vertical relationship between the investigator and God, and the point of every missionary lesson is to help the investigator build his or her own relationship with God. That relationship is the primary source of a complete and authentic testimony. It is also the foundation for the investigator's longer term process of becoming Christ's disciple.

Missionaries initiate that process at the end of the first lesson by inviting the investigator to make two commitments—first, to read in the Book of Mormon, and second, to pray, asking God if the book is true. If the investigator doesn't do those two things, he or she probably won't receive a true testimony. But if he does read and he does pray, he will obtain the kind of testimony that will launch him on the lifelong journey of becoming a true follower, a disciple, of Jesus Christ, following the Son back to the presence of the Father. Everything else the missionaries teach is intended to build that testimony, coaching the investigator along his journey toward God, one step at a time.

Meanwhile, consider the other vertical relationship—the one between the individual missionary and God. The missionary is working every day to strengthen his own testimony, his own discipleship. What Mormon said of himself is true of every missionary and every Church member who accepts some other call to serve: "I am a disciple of Jesus Christ, the Son of God. I have been called of him to declare his word among his people, that they might have everlasting life" (3 Nephi 5:13).

So, in addition to teaching others, a missionary constantly studies, prays, and nourishes his own spiritual growth. That's why chapter 6 of *Preach My Gospel* helps missionaries develop Christlike attributes. They are His followers. Their goal, like that of any disciple, is to become like Him.

Becoming truly consecrated disciples ourselves is the single most important factor in our ability to teach others about following Christ. Whether we are conscious of it or not, we inevitably teach what we are. No wonder Alma said, "Trust no one to be your teacher . . . except he be a man of God, walking in his ways and keeping his commandments" (Mosiah 23:14). This pattern—being a true disciple in order to help others become true disciples—applies not just to missionaries; it is the most basic purpose behind every calling in every Church organization, no matter where a ward or branch is located, and no matter how big it is.

When any servant of the Lord does His work, in any calling, he or she will receive the Lord's pay. What is the Lord's pay?

When he first organized the Church, Alma taught that "the priests were not to depend upon the people for their support; but for their labor they were to receive the grace of God, that they might wax strong in the Spirit, having the knowledge of God, that they might teach with power and authority from God" (Mosiah 18:26).

So the harder we work as His servants, the more the Lord blesses us with His grace, strengthening our own testimony and helping us teach with ever more power and authority—which means that the Lord's greatest pay comes in letting us help someone else. When we, as instruments in the Lord's hands, teach others, we feel the vibrations in our own soul as He plucks our heartstrings to send sounds and signals to those we teach. "Wherefore, he that preacheth and he that receiveth, understand one another, and both are edified and rejoice together" (D&C 50:22).

This same simple triangle could describe parents' teaching relationship with their children. Just put the word *parents* in place of *missionaries* and *child* in place of *investigator*.

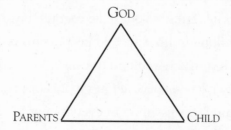

As a parent, I have no more important "investigators" than my children. And the best thing I can do for them is help them develop their own private relationship with the Lord as His true disciples.

The last time I heard President James E. Faust teach the General Authorities, he said that regardless of our other duties, our greatest responsibility and blessing is to raise a righteous posterity. President Faust told us he had just held a new great-granddaughter in his arms. His first thought was, "Will she and I both live long enough that I will have the opportunity to bear my testimony to her?"

Then he recalled his boyhood and his relationship with his own gentle grandfather. He loved to visit his grandfather's ranch, where the two of them would work together with the animals, crops, and fences. At times, his grandfather would teach little Jim some gospel idea and bear his testimony about it in language just right for a boy. Then his grandfather would give him a hug and tell Jim he loved him. President Faust could still remember the feel of the stubble from his grandfather's slight beard against his cheek as they hugged. His grandfather's testimony touched him with a spirit that sparked his own boyish testimony.

Since I shared President Faust's story with Marie, she and I have felt a deeper desire to look upon our children and grandchildren as our most special "investigators." Mixed with the other adventures and good times we share with our lively grandchildren, we pray to find natural, comfortable ways to help them remember our love and our testimonies in the way President Faust always remembered his grandfather.

At the same time, although parents can give their children all kinds of gifts and goods, they cannot give them the parents' own testimony. Parents can teach their children, bear testimony to them, and show them by example the fruits of following Christ in their daily lives. As President Faust's story shows, the teaching and role modeling of parents and grandparents clearly influences their posterity. But ultimately, each child needs to discover and exercise his or her own faith. That's why, as one perceptive friend observed, the Church is always just one generation away from apostasy. You can lead a child to a book, but you can't make him read it. By its very nature, a testimony that is only imposed from the outside is not really a testimony, because it has no internal roots.

In the words of President Thomas S. Monson, "We can rely on the faith and testimony of others only so long. Eventually we must have our own strong and deeply placed foundation, or we will be unable to withstand the storms of life, which *will* come."[2]

A few years ago the Church did some research to see why some active Latter-day Saint youth go on missions and marry in the temple while others (despite having been active in the Church in their younger years) do not. This research found that two factors in a teenager's life were especially influential. First, children whose parents are married in the temple are several times more likely to go on missions and marry in the temple themselves than are children whose parents are not married in the temple. Parental example and teachings do influence a child's convictions.

Second, children whose Church experience includes *private* religious behavior are much more likely one day to go on a mission and marry in the temple than are children who engage only in *public* religious behavior. Private religious behavior includes such practices as personal scripture study and prayer—which establish a real relationship with God, the source of a true, internalized testimony. Young people who experience only public religious behavior—such as Church attendance, social participation, or other public activity—are far less likely to develop the internal motivation that will carry them to the temple. Why is that? The short answer is that just sitting in church won't turn you into a Saint any more than sitting in a garage will turn you into a car.

Laman and Lemuel, for example, had plenty of public religious experience. They sacrificed to follow their parents into the wilderness, they went back to Jerusalem for the plates, and they made the entire journey to the promised land—grumbling and whining all the way, but they did it. At least they didn't give up and run home when they were five miles out of Jerusalem. But they never discovered for themselves "the dealings of that God who had created them" (1 Nephi 2:12). Lehi told them all about God, but all people value what they *discover* far more than what they are simply *told*. Until we find Him for ourselves, we won't have a complete testimony, no matter how strong the testimony of our parents is.

Nephi, on the other hand, discovered a private spiritual world that Laman and Lemuel never chose to find. Nephi wrote that he had "great desires to know of the mysteries of God, wherefore, I did cry unto the Lord; and behold he did visit me, and did soften my heart that I did believe all the words which had been spoken by my father; wherefore, I did not rebel against him like unto my brothers" (1 Nephi 2:16). Nephi and Sam desired and chose to develop their own testimonies, but Laman and Lemuel did not. That one difference among Lehi's sons is the most important distinguishing element in the stories of their lives—and in the lives of their posterity.

I saw an example of a child's private religious life when we visited one of our sons and his wife and family. As Marie and I spent the day in a variety of activities with those grandchildren, one exuberant young grandson volunteered to bless the food at each meal. That night, after Marie had gone with our son and his wife to see their new baby in the hospital, I enjoyed the complete family bedtime routine with the other children.

After they brushed their teeth, put on their pajamas, and sang a song, I read them a story or two. Then I asked the oldest boy to say a family prayer. Once more, his enthusiastic little brother raised his hand and bounced up and down wanting to say the prayer. I must have looked a little perplexed, because the older brother said reassuringly, "Grandpa, it's okay—let him say it."

So the little guy said one more prayer. As I was turning out the light, his older brother came and whispered to me, "Grandpa, it's all right for him to say all the prayers, because after the lights are out, I always say my own prayer by my bed before I go to sleep." That simple communication told me that this young man had already entered Nephi's private spiritual world, and I hugged him in gratitude.

Before we discuss the elements of a complete testimony, let us consider briefly two prerequisites to a testimony: first, desire; and second, worthiness.

If we really want a testimony, we, like Nephi, must *desire* to find God above all other desires. As Alma compared growing a seed with growing a testimony, he said, "Even if ye can no more than desire to believe, let this desire work in you, even until ye believe in a manner that ye can give place for a portion of my words" (Alma 32:27).

Our desires determine our direction. That's why we show what we really want by what we do, not just by what we say. If we say we desire to know Him, but the way we live says otherwise, we probably want something else more. And whatever it is we want so much, we are likely some day to have it. As Lehi taught, we "are free to choose liberty and eternal life" or "captivity and death" and misery, according to our desires (2 Nephi 2:27).

In the long run, then, our most deeply held desires will govern our choices, one by one and day by day, until our lives finally add up to what we have really wanted most—for good or otherwise. We can indeed have eternal life, if we really *want* it, so long as we don't want something else more. In Alma's words, "he that knoweth good and evil, to him it is given according to his desires, whether he desireth good or evil, life or death, joy or remorse of conscience" (Alma 29:5).

Now let us connect desires to worthiness. Because our desires guide and shape our direction, we must be careful during our search for truth to avoid getting hooked on forces that twist our desires. Richard Bushman tells the story of his son's going off to college when he was still unsure about his testimony. Richard encouraged his son to continue his quest for his own witness—on one condition. He asked him to promise that he would keep the commandments while he was searching, because otherwise he would bias his search. Because sin produces guilty feelings, our subconscious self (and the adversary) will try to protect us from the pain of guilt by insisting that the gospel is not true.

Moreover, the Holy Ghost is the ultimate source of the witness we seek, and He cannot be in an unclean place. If we are unworthy, we make Him unwelcome. Notice these three consequences, not only of unclean acts but of unclean thoughts: "He that looketh on a woman to lust after her, or if any shall commit adultery in their hearts, they," first, "shall not have the Spirit"; second, "shall deny the faith"; and third, "shall fear" (D&C 63:16).

Not having the Spirit and denying the faith are exactly the opposite of developing a spiritually grounded testimony. So, lust blocks out testimony. In vivid contrast to the effects of lustful thoughts, notice the three consequences of letting "virtue garnish thy thoughts unceasingly": With virtue rather than lust in our minds, "then shall thy confidence wax strong in the presence of God" (the very opposite of fear), "the doctrine of the priesthood shall distil upon thy soul as the dews from heaven" (the very opposite of denying the faith), and the "Holy Ghost shall be thy constant companion" (the very opposite of not having the Spirit) (D&C 121:45–46).

Brigham Young's plain language put it this way: "Pray the Lord to inspire your hearts. Ask for wisdom and knowledge. It is our duty to seek after it. Let us seek, and we shall find; . . . but as for His coming down here to pour His Spirit upon you, while you are aiming after the vain and frivolous things of the world; indulging in all of the vanity, nonsense, and foolery which surrounds you; drinking in all the filthy abomination which should be spurned from every community on the earth—so long as you continue this course, rest assured He will not come near you."[3]

Chapter 4

REASON, FEELING, AND EXPERIENCE

The three elements that form and support a complete testimony are reason, feeling, and experience. I draw again on the metaphor of a triangle to show how these elements interconnect, because each side of a triangle strengthens the other two sides:

"If there is a single most important shape in engineering, it is the triangle. Unlike a rectangle, a triangle cannot be deformed without changing the length of one of its sides or breaking one of its joints. In fact, one of the simplest ways to strengthen a rectangle is to add supports that form triangles at the rectangle's corners or across its diagonal length. A single support between two diagonal corners greatly strengthens a rectangle by turning it into two triangles."[1]

This image is especially fitting to suggest how the three parts of a testimony reinforce each other. Put together with its three strong corners in place, the triangle of testimony is anchored and sure.

I am struck by the similarity between the process of developing a testimony and the process of falling in love. Love and testimony are two of the most important human experiences, yet often we are unsure how to be certain that either has come fully into our lives. It helps me to realize that each process builds on the same component parts—the three sides of the reason-feeling-experience triangle.

In finding the love we seek during our courtship years, we often have in mind the personal qualities we are looking for. But even when we meet someone who has everything on our list of qualities (let's call that the test of reason), there may be some "spark" missing—that mysterious something that lets us *feel* love, not just think it (let's call that the test of feeling).

Yet rational satisfaction and good feelings are still not enough. To know if we're really in love, we need a little testing time (call it the test of experience). We can't tell the difference between one thin strand from a cobweb and one thin strand from a powerful cable just by looking at them. We need to see what happens when we put stress on the strand. To know if what we're thinking and feeling is love, not just infatuation, we must see how a relationship holds up under stress, whether it grows and stirs, whether it takes on a life of its own. And the process of searching for a testimony is very similar to the process of searching to know when we're in love.

Consider now each side of the triangle of testimony. We begin with reason, or the thoughts in our minds. In describing "the spirit of revelation," the Lord said, "Yea, behold, I will tell you *in your mind* and in your heart, by the Holy Ghost, which shall come upon you and which shall dwell in your heart" (D&C 8:2; emphasis added). Joseph Smith

once said that we may notice "the first intimation of the spirit of revelation" when we "feel pure intelligence flowing into [our minds;] it may
give [us] sudden strokes of ideas."[2] The Lord told Oliver Cowdery, "You
have not understood; you have supposed that I would give it unto you,
when you took no thought save it was to ask me. But, behold, . . . you
must study it out in your mind; then you must ask me if it be right"
(D&C 9:7–8). In other words, do your homework first. Then feelings
and experience can come along to confirm your reasoning.

In a more general sense, a religious explanation for life actually
makes more sense rationally than does an atheistic or agnostic explanation. I am impatient with shallow skeptics who say that religious truth
must be taken solely on faith, as if no rational evidence for religious
propositions exists—and as if no scientific propositions are taken on
faith. When Lehi and Nephi in the book of Helaman had great missionary success, Moroni tells us that "the more part of the Lamanites
were convinced [that their message was true] because of the greatness
of the *evidences* which they had received" (Helaman 5:50; emphasis
added).

Alma told the skeptical Korihor, "All things denote there is a God;
yea, even the earth, and all things that are upon the face of it, yea, and
its motion" (Alma 30:44). Science tells us that if the earth were even
slightly nearer to the sun, all life here would burn up. If the sun were
even slightly farther away, all life here would freeze. As I see the
destructive power of a tsunami, or a hurricane, or an earthquake, I see
no way that we could carry on life as we do if the elements were not

held in check by divine laws and powers. If we were truly at the mercy of arbitrary natural forces, wind and sand and tidal waves would knock this planet around like a leaf in a storm.

As for whether God is our Creator, I like the question someone asked: "What are the odds that a tornado spinning through a junkyard would create a Boeing 747?"

It really is more consistent with the scientific evidence to believe in a divine Creator than not to believe in Him. The acclaimed biologist Francis Collins developed that point in a recent *New York Times* best-seller, *The Language of God: A Scientist Presents Evidence for Belief.* Collins led the International Human Genome Project, which in 2000 announced that its team had put together the first complete map of the entire human DNA code. Seeing that complex code as "the language in which God created life," Collins shows that "belief in God can be an entirely rational choice, and that the principles of faith are, in fact, complementary with the principles of science."

Collins writes that the earth exhibits in just the right proportions all of fifteen scientific "physical constants" that are necessary to sustain its complex life forms. The likelihood that this unique combination could come together by sheer chance "is almost infinitesimal. . . . In sum, [without God] our universe is wildly improbable."[3] Thus, "faith in God [is] more rational than disbelief."[4]

Regarding the Restoration, rational evidence that supports Joseph Smith's claims grows stronger every day. For example, when he announced the Word of Wisdom, neither Joseph nor anyone else knew that tobacco causes lung cancer. Consider as well Joseph's prophecy about where the Civil War would begin, or his prophecy that the restored Church would fill North and South America.

Think of Joseph's calling as a prophet while he was such a young man. Within the accepted framework of biblical history, there was nothing unusual about angels appearing to an inexperienced boy as part of a prophetic call. However, one skeptic I know regards the First Vision as "so unlikely." Others reflect the narrow lens of their modern secularism by saying, "We just don't get books from angels." But if the Bible is evidence for anything, read about the callings of Noah, Abraham, Moses, Isaac, Jacob, Samuel, Isaiah, Jeremiah, Paul, and John the Revelator. All were called by direct heavenly manifestations. All spoke with God or angels, just as Joseph did.

Consider also the growing body of research that authenticates many ancient practices and other facts in the Book of Mormon, on subjects ranging from the Nephite legal system to geography. Studies by Latter-day Saint scholars on word prints show that the Book of Mormon could not have been written by only one author.

Also, consider the Hebrew poetry form called chiasmus, as clear a pattern as a limerick or iambic pentameter in English. Nobody in the United States had heard of chiasmus in Joseph's day. But, thanks to the work of today's LDS researchers, we now know that this striking literary form is scattered throughout the Book of Mormon. Anyone who diagrams the entire chapter of Alma 36 according to chiastic form is in for a stunning and reassuring surprise. Those who wrote on the golden plates had educated Hebrew origins, so they knew and used Hebrew literary forms. But Joseph Smith may not even have known he was translating poetic forms.

LDS scholars have now established enough of a track record that they have shifted the momentum of critical debate in the Church's favor. For example, a few years ago, two Protestant scholars visited Brigham Young University on a research project related to the Dead Sea Scrolls, in which BYU has played a major role. They later presented a paper to their evangelical colleagues expressing their great concern that evangelicals underestimate the strength of Mormon scholarship. They warned their colleagues that it was a "myth" to assume "that when Mormons receive training in historiography, biblical languages, theology, and philosophy they invariably abandon traditional Latter-day Saints (LDS) beliefs." They concluded that there are indeed "legitimate Mormon scholars . . . 'skilled in intellectual investigation, trained in ancient languages'" who "are not an anti-intellectual group." Further, "Mormon scholars . . . have, with varying degrees of success, answered most of the usual evangelical criticisms."

These Protestant scholars continued: "Currently there are . . . no books from an evangelical perspective that responsibly interact with contemporary LDS scholarly and apologetic writings. A survey of twenty recent evangelical books criticizing Mormonism reveals that *none* interacts with this growing body of literature. Only a handful demonstrate any awareness of pertinent works. Many of the authors promote criticisms that have long been refuted. A number of these books claim to be 'the definitive' book on the matter. That they make no attempt to interact with contemporary LDS scholarship is a stain upon the authors' integrity and causes one to wonder about their credibility.

" . . . at the academic level, evangelicals are needlessly losing the debate with the Mormons. In recent years the sophistication and erudition of LDS [scholarship] has risen considerably while evangelical responses have not." Moreover, these evangelical scholars said, "In this battle the Mormons are fighting valiantly. And the evangelicals? It appears that we may be losing the battle and not knowing it."[5]

Of course, as Elder Neal A. Maxwell once said, "Science will not be able to prove or disprove holy writ. However, enough plausible evidence" supporting the Book of Mormon "will come forth to prevent scoffers from having a field day, but not enough to remove the requirement of faith."[6] As C. S. Lewis scholar Austin Farrer put it, "Rational argument does not create belief, but it maintains a climate in which belief may flourish."[7]

Science and history never do lead to absolute conclusions about religion. By their nature, science and history are always subject to new evidence and new interpretations of old evidence. Thus, if our testimonies are based completely on empirical evidence or rational analysis, they can still be more like cobwebs than like cables. Reason isn't enough by itself to overcome the full power of temptation or prejudice.

A testimony therefore needs the second side of the triangle— spiritual feelings from the Holy Ghost. The scriptures are full of references to the influence of the Spirit on our feelings. Alma speaks of "when you *feel* these swelling motions," *in addition* to the more rational experience of discovering that truth can "enlighten [our] understanding" (Alma 32:28; emphasis added). Nephi talks to his brothers about being past feeling and chastises them because they refused to feel the Spirit's words (1 Nephi 17:45).

Moroni explains that the Holy Ghost will manifest the truth of the Book of Mormon if we pray with a sincere heart and real intent—*after* doing our homework (Moroni 10:4–5). Nephi tells us that the Holy Ghost carries His power to the hearts of the children of men (2 Nephi 33:1; D&C 8:2). So the men who talked with the resurrected Christ without recognizing Him on the road to Emmaus said afterward, when they realized who He was, "Did not our heart burn within us, while he talked with us by the way . . . ?" (Luke 24:32).

This description echoes the Lord's words to Oliver Cowdery regarding the translation process. After Oliver had studied the process in his own mind, he was to ask the Lord. "And if it is right I will cause that your bosom shall burn within you; therefore, you shall *feel* that it is right" (D&C 9:8; emphasis added).

The Spirit can also convey a feeling of peace rather than a feeling of burning. On another occasion, the Lord told Oliver, "Cast your mind upon the night that you cried unto me in your heart, that you might know concerning the truth of these things. Did I not speak peace to your mind concerning the matter? What greater witness can you have than from God?" (D&C 6:22–23).

I'll always remember the night when, as a new missionary, I first became aware of the Holy Ghost bearing witness to a sincere investigator. As my companion bore his testimony to her about the Resurrection, tears filled her eyes, and I felt that my heart would burst from the overflowing of spiritual warmth. Afterward I asked my companion if he had felt anything unusual during our discussion. He smiled and asked, "Do you know what that was?" Then, recognizing this was a new but very important experience for me, he said, "Elder Hafen, that was the Holy Ghost bearing witness of the truth. There is no other feeling quite like that. We may not feel it often. You can't turn it off and on like a water tap. But when it comes, you begin to recognize what it is."

Years after that missionary experience, I found myself teaching one of our children just what my companion had taught me about the Spirit. We were gathered at a family barbeque at their grandparents' house. Chunks of hamburger buns and chips were strewn around the backyard. After dinner, Grandpa invited everyone to go into the living room and sit down. As the crowd of young grandchildren trooped into the house, something caught their spiritual attention, and all became very quiet.

Grandpa stood in the center of the room, supporting himself with the back of a chair. He told us that he had been having trouble recovering from a recent hip surgery and would like a priesthood blessing. This father of five daughters asked his sons-in-law to anoint and bless him. We surrounded his chair and performed the ordinance with great love and respect for him.

Then he thanked the whole family for their prayers, adding some brief words of testimony to his posterity. He said that all he ever wanted after he died was to live with the very people who were in that room. He seemed quietly majestic as he spoke to us. Then he was finished. No song. No prayer. Everyone just began moving around quietly to clean up the yard and the kitchen.

Our twelve-year-old son approached me, wanting to talk. He wasn't easily given to expressing personal feelings, but he did that day. He brushed away tears and asked, "Dad, what's the matter with me? Why am I crying? I'm not sad—I'm happy that Grandpa could have a blessing. I just love him and I want him to get better."

I said, "Why don't you go tell him that?"

He ran to his grandpa and hugged him. They exchanged a few words, and he came back to me, even more visibly affected but still puzzled. Then I told him, as my missionary companion had told me years earlier, that he was sensing the Holy Ghost. He was also feeling love and appreciation for the priesthood, and the Spirit was telling him that what he sensed was true and good. In this rare teaching moment, I urged him never to forget what this felt like, because he was feeling the Lord's Spirit.

When I was younger, I somehow had the impression that spiritual feelings were not recognized outside the religious sphere as a legitimate source of knowledge. I have since discovered that inner sight, or inspiration, is an established way of learning. The premises from which scientists reason must come from some source. Those thoughts may come from previous experiments, they might come from personal intuition, or they may indeed come from a divine source. The Book of Mormon tells us that one of history's most celebrated explorers, Christopher Columbus, was directed by "the Spirit of God," which "came down and wrought upon the man" (1 Nephi 13:12).

The German composer Johannes Brahms vividly described the inspired feelings that came to him during the creative process of writing fine music: "I immediately feel vibrations that thrill my whole being. . . . These are the Spirit illuminating the soul-power within, and . . . I feel capable of drawing inspiration from above. . . .

"Straightway the ideas flow in upon me, directly from God, and not only do I see distinct themes in my mind's eye, but they are clothed in the right forms, harmonies and orchestration."

At the same time, Brahms realized that his efforts required great skill and exertion: "Don't make the mistake of thinking that because I attach such importance to inspiration from above, that that is all there is to it, by no means. Structure is just as consequential, for without craftsmanship, inspiration is as sounding brass."

But because inspiration gives the best music its highest power, Brahms declared, the work of "composers who are atheists" is "doomed to speedy oblivion, because they are utterly lacking in inspiration."[8]

So there will be both *reason* and inspired *feelings* in our experiences with testimony. Yet we know that even spiritual feelings can be forgotten and that sometimes we may confuse lesser emotions with truly inspired impressions. Further, our feelings can sometimes be influenced by unwise people who would manipulate them.

Our triangle of testimony needs one last side to stabilize its total support structure—a side we will simply call experience. Our understanding of truth needs an incubation period, a chance to settle in and take root, just as Alma describes in Alma 32. This is the test of time, the season when we nourish and water the seed we have planted. We must also overcome the opposition and hazards we face after the seed takes root and sprouts, when the sun's heat can scorch the tender plant.

Alma also teaches about the interactive relationship between faith and knowledge as time goes on. When experience confirms our earliest impressions, we are still not in an "either/or" place, where we either "know" everything or just "believe" everything. We experience elements of both knowledge and belief. In the beginning of the process, Alma says we "cannot know" of the "surety" of God's words at first, for we completely lack experience (Alma 32:26). At that stage, we follow our desires as an act of faith. After doing that, we can testify of what we have learned experientially, for our "knowledge [has become] perfect in that thing" (Alma 32:34). We can then stand on that base of knowledge as we take another step of faith, which will lead us to expand our knowledge.

For instance, those who pay tithing when it would seem they cannot afford it are often blessed with new ideas about managing their money; and suddenly they discover something that those who don't pay tithing cannot understand. From this foundation, they can step up to other acts of faith, knowing with new confidence that God keeps His promises.

During my own experience as a missionary, Alma's words took on vivid meaning for me, showing me that gaining a testimony is usually a process, not just a one-time event. Moreover, faith plus action leads to knowledge. That's why Brigham Young said that "more testimonies are obtained on the feet than on the knees."[9]

In the years before my mission, I was somewhat stuck on the difference between "knowing" and "believing." I earnestly believed in the gospel—enough to accept a mission call—but I couldn't understand how others could say they "knew" it was true. In my sacrament meeting talk just before I left for my mission, I couldn't say I *knew*, only that I *believed*. Within a few months, however, I would learn for myself what it meant to know.

I had accepted Alma's invitation to experiment, letting my desire to believe work in me enough to nourish his words like a seed. Moroni's words also rang true to me during those days: "Dispute not because ye see not, for ye receive no witness until after the trial of your faith" (Ether 12:6).

I mentioned earlier the first time I realized that the Holy Ghost was bearing witness to our investigator. Soon afterward came another experience in my own growth process. During an all-mission conference in Frankfurt, Germany, then-Elder Harold B. Lee quoted to us from Doctrine and Covenants 46 on spiritual gifts: "To some it is given by the Holy Ghost to know that Jesus Christ is the Son of God" and "to others it is given to believe on their words, that they also might have eternal life if they continue faithful" (vv. 13–14).

He then bore a stirring witness that he had received the gift to know

of Christ's divinity. He invited us to believe him and lean on his testimony. Instantly, a new thought was very clear to me: I knew that he knew.
And somehow that added something important to my own testimony.

After that came many other experiences that taught me how the
sprouting seed grows its roots of knowledge in the soil of experience.
For example, in the Frankfurt train station my companion and I met a
young American military couple named Paul and Wendy Knaupp. As
we taught them the missionary discussions, I was impressed with the
light in both their souls.

Years later, Wendy wrote about her first visit with us: "I will always
remember the feeling I had when I first heard the Joseph Smith story!
I can picture our tiny upstairs German apartment that was probably as
big as our bedroom today, with us sitting on the edge of the bed/couch
[facing the missionaries]. I had always felt that there must be something
like [the missionaries' message] out there somewhere. It seemed so right
and I believed it."

Soon after deciding to be baptized, however, Wendy and Paul heard
from a family member who criticized the Church's policy about not giving the priesthood to those of African descent. They became confused
and discouraged. They asked us not to come again, except once more to
say good-bye. We fasted and we prayed, knowing we had only one last
chance. As we sat down and began to talk, I worried that I didn't know
at all what I should say. Then I suddenly felt prompted to read with them
a scripture I had noticed for the first time several weeks earlier in my personal study, the story of Peter and Cornelius in Acts 10–11.

This story recounts the historic moment when God gave Peter the revelation that the gospel should be taken to the Gentiles, after having been restricted to blood Israel throughout the Old Testament and the life of Christ. I had never heard anyone respond to Paul and Wendy's question with that scripture, but that is what came to my mind. The story showed us that it wasn't historically correct to say that God had always treated every race the same. The revelation to Peter also shows that God can and will give new light through continuing revelation, as occurred through the revelation to President Spencer W. Kimball on this same subject in 1978.

That night I realized a fulfillment of the Lord's promise to missionaries: "Treasure up in your minds continually the words of life" (D&C 84:85) and "it shall be given you in the very hour, yea, in the very moment, what ye shall say" and "the Holy Ghost shall [bear] record unto all things whatsoever ye shall say" (D&C 100:6, 8). We all felt a spirit of peace as we prayed.

Years later Wendy wrote her memory of that evening: "I don't remember what [the missionaries] told us, but that light . . . the Spirit . . . was back and I knew that it was true, and even though I didn't understand [completely, the message] was still true and we needed to accept it, and at some future time we would come to understand." Paul and Wendy were baptized and have raised five children, all of whom are now active in the Church.

What happened to me that night was so tangible and so significant for Paul and Wendy that I didn't just believe the Lord had helped us—

I knew it, because I had experienced it. So I knew exactly what Alma meant when he asked, "Is not this real?" (Alma 32:35). In the decades that followed, I also tasted the precious fruit from Alma's tree as I watched the gospel's teachings richly bless the members of Paul and Wendy's family.

To illustrate further the power of experience, I go back to the missionary I met in the airport (see page 39). He did return home early from his mission, for a variety of reasons. I met with him several months after his return and found him to be a worthy and honest young man. During that visit, I learned that he had experienced some misguided years in his late teens. Like the prodigal son, he had learned the hard way that he would be much happier if he returned to Church activity—and so he did. He then undertook a thorough process of repentance and decided on his own to serve a mission. Since returning home, he had remained active in the Church, though he was still unclear about his testimony.

I asked if he felt that the Lord had influenced his decision to change his life and then to serve a mission. "Yes, of course," he said. Then he expressed his deep personal gratitude for the Savior's Atonement. He added that he'd also had some spiritual guidance recently in ending a relationship with a young woman, which, he said, was a good thing. Then he expressed his desire to find a new companion and marry her in the temple.

As we looked back together on his life, I asked if he could see the answers to any prayers in what he had experienced since those hard teen years. He quietly said again, "Of course."

"Sounds like the beginnings of a real testimony to me," I said.

He smiled a little and nodded. He was beginning to know that he knew.

I offer one more example of how experience has contributed to my own testimony. We have recently enjoyed a number of visits with our seven married children and their children, after having been in Europe for a few years on a Church assignment. I have been amazed and humbled by seeing the long-term fruits of the gospel in the lives of our children, their wonderfully faithful spouses, and now their own children.

When our children were young, there were days when I really wondered if all of our family home evenings and other homemade efforts were making any difference. Once our bishop affectionately referred to our busy little brood, crowded onto a bench at church, as "the Hafen children—curtain climbers, rug rats, and house apes." But a generation later, I can only quote the hymn: "Count your many blessings"—just look around you—"and it will surprise you what the Lord has done."[10]

Each of our grandchildren has a unique personality, but in each young countenance is a certain familiar light. Each of their families has its own style, and none of them is perfect. But all are blessed with a similar blend of love, discipline, goodness, cooperation, and spiritual security. That blend is creating a consistent pattern across all seven families.

I have seen that same blend in the homes of faithful Latter-day

Saints around the world. If the gospel is a real force in a family's daily walk and conversation, and if they honestly seek to live what Nephi called "after the manner of happiness" (2 Nephi 5:27), the result is like seeing clothing made from the same pattern or delicious dinners made from the same recipe—regardless of culture or language.

The gospel works when we work to live it, despite the occasional exceptions and the normal ups and downs of everyday life. Then the Lord's promised fruits appear on the tree of life in the family garden, because each tree sprouted and grew from the same kind of seed. "By their fruits ye shall know them" (3 Nephi 14:20; Matthew 7:20). What I have seen in my own children's lives is evidence of the gospel's truth that I would gladly put on the witness stand in a court of law.

I could tell many more stories that have brought my testimony through the tests of reason, feeling, and experience stretched over the years. A testimony really does live and grow organically, like a seed that becomes a tree, and the tree eventually bears precious fruit. I am now in the stage of life where I taste that fruit often enough that I am overwhelmed with wonder, rather than wondering if what I am tasting is real.

With the same honesty that once kept me from being able to say "I know," I can now say what Elder Harold B. Lee said to our mission years ago: It really has been given to me "by the Holy Ghost to know that Jesus Christ is the Son of God" (D&C 46:13). That knowledge is not simply the result of one dramatic event; rather, it is the aggregate conclusion from many thoughts, feelings, and experiences in a lifelong process. I know that Christ lives. I know that His gospel is true.

Part III

LOVE IS
NOT BLIND

Chapter 5

WHEN THINGS SEEM UNCERTAIN

When we are young, most of us tend to think in terms of black and white—there is very little gray in either the intellectual or spiritual dimension of our perspective. So most young adults have a childlike optimism and loyalty that make them wonderfully teachable. It is typical of students at Latter-day Saint colleges, for example, to trust their teachers, to believe what they read, and to respond with enthusiasm to invitations for Church service.

New converts to the Church often have similar attitudes, which help them make a refreshing contribution to their wards and branches as their optimistic spirit and outlook influence those who have been in the Church for many years.

Where else but in a college student ward would you find a Church member so thrilled to be called by the bishop as the hymnbook coordinator or the refreshment specialist for ward socials? As an older student at Brigham Young University told me, one thing he likes about being in a student ward composed mostly of freshmen and sophomores is that when topics such as faith or repentance are raised for discussion, nobody yawns.

The Gospel Essentials class in many wards has a similar feel, because it is attended mostly by new members, investigators, and those returning to Church activity, who all tend to share an engaging freshness as they study the gospel.

As time goes on, however, experience often introduces a new dimension to the perspective of younger and newer Church members. This new dimension is typically a growing awareness of a kind of gap between the real and the ideal—between what *is* and what *ought* to be.

One way of describing this gap is to imagine two circles, one inside the other. The inner boundary is "the real," or what is. The outer boundary is "the ideal," or what ought to be. We stand at the inner boundary of reality, reaching out to move our reality closer to our lofty ideals. We first see the distance between these two boundaries when we realize that some things about ourselves or about other Church members are not what we expected—or what we wish they were. That realization can naturally produce some frustration.

Our experience with the Church, or with Church institutions, can make us a little vulnerable to the questions this gap can raise—in part because our idealistic expectations may be very high. A new Church member, for example, is accustomed to receiving frequent—sometimes almost daily—visits from the missionaries who first taught him or her the gospel. But within a few weeks after baptism, the missionaries probably aren't visiting as often, because they spend most of their time with investigators, and the newly assigned home or visiting teachers may miss a few visits. This unexpected decline in personal support may make it harder for a new convert to keep the commitments that asked for major lifestyle changes—which is one reason why strong ward priesthood and auxiliary leaders work hard to increase their own support for new members.

Similarly, a new BYU student may find it a bit lonely and frustrating to be one among thirty thousand students, fighting occasional battles with the red-tape machine that seems to control the processes of admission, registering for classes, or transferring credits from another school. A student in his first few weeks of school may feel unknown and nameless to the bishop of a student ward who is flooded with many new ward members all at once. Or he may brush up against a faculty member whose attitudes about the Church are more flexible (or more rigid) than he had expected them to be.

At a more personal level, perhaps an important prayer goes too long unanswered, or one suffers a surprise health setback or an unexpected conflict with a family member. Perhaps one becomes conscious of the imperfections of other Church members and leaders or of one's own parents. When we become acquainted at an adult level with those who have been our heroes and our trusted friends, we naturally begin to see their human limitations. Perhaps one encounters some anti-Mormon literature, or one discovers differing views about the Church among its members and leaders. We may also find ourselves looking for more complete ways to clarify the previously unarticulated assumptions behind our testimonies, which were perhaps based mostly on spiritual feelings. As Peter said, "Be ready always to give . . . a reason of the hope that is in you" (1 Peter 3:15).

New missionaries may discover a jarring sense of distance between the real and the ideal as they move from the "premortal realm" of the Missionary Training Center to the "mortality" of daily life in an assigned field of missionary service. I vividly recall my feelings of great discouragement during my first few weeks as a missionary in a foreign country. I had studied the language in college, but hearing the natives speak their mother tongue at first sounded incomprehensible to me; I understood virtually nothing and was literally speechless for the first time I could remember.

Even after the language began to make sense, I repeatedly fought back tears of disappointment when in various parts of our work, the promised fruits of a positive mental attitude seemed frequently to elude me.

I recall, for instance, my feelings of disbelief and pain one night when we had an appointment to make final plans for the baptismal service of a young couple I had considered truly golden investigators. They had responded positively to each lesson we taught, they had attended church, and they were reading and praying about the Book of Mormon with very believing attitudes. But that night, as we rang the doorbell, someone turned out the lights inside their apartment. We rang again. Nothing.

In disbelief, we stepped away from the door and called through their window, "It's us—the missionaries! We're here to see you!" No answer came. My companion and I looked at each other and then began to cry as we trudged together back to our bicycles. I knew there was some untold story behind their behavior, but that didn't help. I later learned that it was not that unusual to lose progressing investigators with no explanation.

There is a kind of poignancy in those moments when we first discover there might be some limitations to the idea that we can do anything we make up our mind to do. I once gave everything I had to that proposition in my determination to be the greatest shot-putter in the history of my junior high school. But I simply wasn't big enough. It really was hopeless.

Experiences like these can produce uncertainty and ambivalence—in a word, ambiguity—and we may yearn for simpler, easier times, when life was more clear and more under our control. We might sense within ourselves the beginnings of skepticism, of unwillingness to respond to authority or to invitations to commit ourselves to high-sounding goals or projects that don't seem very realistic.

Not everybody will encounter what I have been describing, and I don't mean to suggest that everyone must encounter such experiences. However, many Church members do run into at least some forms of ambiguity sooner or later. (It helps me understand the word *ambiguity* to consider its German translation—*zweideutig,* meaning "capable of meaning two different things.")

The basic teachings of the restored gospel are potent, clear, and unambiguous. But it is possible on occasion to encounter some uncertainty even in studying the scriptures. Consider, for example, the story of Nephi when he killed Laban in order to obtain the brass plates (1 Nephi 4). That case is not easy to interpret until the reader realizes that God Himself, who gave the original commandment against murder, was also the source of Nephi's instructions in that very exceptional case.

Consider also the case of Peter on the night he denied any knowledge of his Master three times in succession (Matthew 26). We typically regard Peter as fearful or, perhaps, weak. We assume his commitment was not strong enough to make him rise to the Savior's defense. But I once heard President Spencer W. Kimball offer an alternative interpretation of Peter's behavior. Then-Elder Kimball suggested that the Savior's statement that Peter would deny him three times before the cock crowed just might have been a request to Peter, not a prediction. Jesus might have been instructing His chief Apostle to deny any association with Him in order to ensure continued leadership for the Church after the Crucifixion.[1]

As Elder Kimball asked his audience, who could doubt Peter's willingness to stand up and be counted? Think of his boldness in striking off the guard's ear with his sword when the Savior was arrested in Gethsemane. Elder Kimball didn't offer this view as the only interpretation, but he said there is enough basis for it that it should be considered. So what is the correct answer—was Peter a coward, or was he so crucial to the survival of the Church that he was prohibited from risking his life? We are not sure. The scriptures don't give us enough information about Peter's motivation to clarify the ambiguity.

Consider other examples from the scriptures. The Lord has said that He cannot look upon sin with the least degree of allowance (D&C 1:31). Yet elsewhere He has said, "I have forgiven you your sins" (D&C 64:3) and "Neither do I condemn thee: go, and sin no more" (John 8:11). Justice is indeed a divine law, but so is the principle of mercy. At times these two correct principles can seem inconsistent, until the unifying higher doctrine of the Atonement brings them together.

These references illustrate that even though God has given us correct principles by which we may govern ourselves, these very principles may at times be in conflict. Choosing between two principled alternatives (two "goods") is more difficult than choosing when we see a stark and obvious contrast between good and evil.

We often face competition between true principles, such as when we are trying to fulfill our duties to family, Church, and profession. I remember a young mother who had a large family, a responsible Church calling, and a busy husband. She expressed her bewilderment about trying to decide what should come first in her life and when. Someone advised her, "Well, just be sure you put the Lord's work first." Her reply was, "But what if it is *all* the Lord's work?"

During our young parenting years, Marie and I were at times perplexed about how to deal with our children in some circumstance that hadn't been anticipated in anything we had ever heard or read about child-rearing. At times one of us had a clear feeling about what to do, but sometimes we had no idea what approach was best—so we prayed often for help. Once we asked a friend for advice about a vexing question. He wasn't very helpful when he simply said with great conviction, "Well, just be sure you do the right thing."

Church and family life are not the only topics where the right answer is not always on the tip of our tongues. To stretch our minds about the implications of uncertainty and differences of opinion among Church members, we have only to ask about the recent war in Iraq. With the hindsight of a few years, do we see that war as a mistake, or was it a heroic act of liberating a nation? Or consider whether we should sell everything except what is truly necessary for our survival and donate our surplus to those with far greater needs than ours. Especially amid the current global economic chaos, we might also ask how much governmental intervention in business and private life is too much—or not enough.

The people on the extreme sides of such questions often seem very certain about the right answer. But some people would rather be certain than right.

We might encounter the naturalness of ambiguity in literature. Arthur Henry King, then a literature teacher at Brigham Young University, said that most truly great literary works raise a profound question about a human problem, explore the question skillfully and in depth, and leave the matter for the reader to resolve. He added that

if the resolution seems too clear or too easy, the literature is perhaps
not very good or those reading it have missed its point.

Dostoevsky's novel *The Idiot*, for example, seriously raises the question
whether it is possible for a true Christian to love unselfishly. The
story's main character is a pure and good Christian who loves two different women in two very different ways. One he loves as most men
love women—she cares for him, she helps him, he is attracted to her
romantically, and she could make his life very happy. The other woman
is a pathetically inadequate, dependent person. He loves her primarily
because she needs him so much, and he has a compassionate heart.

Posing the dilemma of which woman the man should marry,
Dostoevsky asks whether it is realistically possible to be totally devoted
to the unselfish ideals of Christianity. He leaves that huge question
unresolved, forcing the reader to ponder it for himself.

Life is full of ambiguities, perhaps because some uncertainty is characteristic of the mortal experience. The mists of darkness in Lehi's
dream are, for that very reason, a strong symbolic representation of life
as we face it on this planet (1 Nephi 8:23). Thankfully, many things in
mortality are very certain and very clear, as so beautifully represented
by the iron rod in Lehi's dream (v. 19). But enough complexity pricks
and pokes at us to make the topic of dealing with uncertainty at least
worth discussing.

Given, then, the existence of a gap for most of us between where
we stand and where we would like to be, and given that we will have at

least some experiences that make us wonder what to do, I suggest three ascending levels of dealing with ambiguity.

At level one, I've noticed two typical attitudes. One of them is that we simply do not—perhaps cannot—even see the problems that exist. Some people seem almost consciously to filter out any perception of a gap between the real and the ideal. For them, the gospel at its best is a firm handshake, an enthusiastic greeting, and a smiley button. Their mission was the best, their ward is the best, and every new day is probably going to be the best day they ever had. These cheerful ones are happy, spontaneous, optimistic, and they always manage to hang loose and relax. They are able to weather many storms that seem formidable to more pessimistic types, though one wonders if they have somehow missed hearing that a storm is going on.

A second group at level one has quite a different problem with the gap between what is and what ought to be. This group eliminates the frustrating distance between the real and the ideal by, in effect, erasing the inner circle of reality—and thereby removing the gap. They cling to the ideal so single-mindedly that they just don't feel the frustration that would come from facing the real facts, perhaps about themselves, about others, or about the world around them. I have sometimes heard from people in this group when reading letters to the editor in the school newspaper at a Church college. They are sometimes quite shocked to discover that some person or some part of the institution has seemed to fall short of perfection.

Those in this group struggle to distinguish between imperfections that matter a great deal and those that may not matter so much. Perhaps Hugh Nibley had them in mind when he spoke of those who find it better to get up at 5:00 A.M. to write a bad book than to get up at 9:00 A.M. to write a good book. While self-discipline is a virtue, Brother Nibley didn't think the exact hour when we arise is quite as important as what we do once we are up.

I recall listening to a group of Church members who discussed which of the two types of people just described offered the best model for their emulation. They felt they had to choose between being relaxed, carefree, and happy about everything in life and being an intense, uncompromising perfectionist. As I listened, I began to see that both categories suffer from the same limitation. It isn't much of a choice when we must select between a forced superficial happiness and a frantic concern with apparent perfection.

Both perspectives lack depth; they understand things too quickly, and they draw conclusions from their experience too easily. Neither is well prepared for adversity, and I fear that the first strong wind that comes along will blow them over. I believe this is primarily because their roots have not sunk far enough into the soil of experience to establish a firm foundation. Both also reflect the thinness of a philosophy that is untempered by simple common sense. In both cases, it would be helpful just to be more realistic about the way life is, even if that means facing some questions and limitations that may make us feel a little uncomfortable. That very discomfort can motivate us to lean into the wind and experience some real growth. As President

Harold B. Lee occasionally said, the true Church is intended not only to comfort the afflicted but to afflict the comfortable.

We should then step up to level two, where we see things for what they are. Only then can we deal with reality in a meaningful and constructive way.

If we are not willing to grapple with the frustration that comes from facing bravely the uncertainties we encounter, we may never develop the spiritual maturity necessary to reach our ultimate destination. Heber C. Kimball said that the Church has yet to pass through some very close places, and those who are living on "borrowed light"—the testimonies of other people—will not be able to stand when those days come.[2]

So we need to develop the ability to form judgments of our own about the value of ideas, opportunities, or people who may come into our lives. We won't always have the security of knowing whether a certain idea is "Church approved," because new ideas don't always come along with little tags attached saying they have been reviewed at Church headquarters. Whether in music, books, friends, or opportunities to serve, there is much that is lovely, of good report, and praiseworthy that is not the subject of detailed discussion in Church manuals, conference talks, or courses of instruction. Those who are not open to people or experiences that are not obviously related to some Church word or program may well live less abundant lives, and make fewer contributions, than the Lord intends.

We must develop enough independence and judgment that we

are ready for the shafts and whirlwinds of adversity and contradiction that may come to us. When those times come, we cannot be living on borrowed light. We should not be deceived by the clear-cut labels others may use to describe circumstances that are, in fact, not so clear. Our encounters with reality and disappointment are actually vital stages in the development of our maturity and understanding.

Chapter 6

BEYOND AMBIGUITY

Despite the value of a level-two awareness, however, there are some serious hazards at this stage. One's acceptance of the clouds of uncertainty may become so complete that the iron rod seems to fade into the blurring mists of darkness, and skepticism becomes a guiding philosophy. Often, this perspective comes from erasing the *outer* circle—representing the ideal, or what ought to be—and then focusing excessively on the inner circle of reality.

During my years of teaching at the Brigham Young University law school, I noticed how common it was for first-year law students to experience frustration when they discovered that our legal system is characterized not by hard and fast rules but by legal principles that often appear to contradict each other.

I recall one new student who approached me after class to express the confusion he was feeling about his study of the law. He said he had what he called "a low tolerance for ambiguity." Part of his challenge, he said, was that only weeks before he had returned from a mission, where everything was crisp and clear, and most of the ideas he expressed to investigators were drawn from an approved set of lesson materials. To feel successful, all he needed to do was follow the step-by-step plan given for each day and each task on his mission. But law school was making him feel totally at sea, as he groped for simple guidelines that would tell him what to do.

By the time our law students reached their third year of study, however, some of them had developed such a high tolerance for ambiguity that they were skeptical about everything. Where formerly they felt they had all the answers but just didn't know what the questions were, now they seemed to have all of the questions but few of the answers.

I tried to tell our graduating law students that people who take too much delight in their finely honed tools of skepticism and dispassionate analysis will limit their effectiveness in law practice, at home, in church, and elsewhere—because they can become contentious, standoffish, arrogant, and unwilling to commit themselves. I have seen some of them try out their new intellectual tools in a Church classroom. When a well-meaning teacher makes a point that the skeptic considers a little silly, the skeptic yields to an irresistible urge to leap to his feet and publicly deflate the teacher's momentum.

If they are successful, these overly analytical types begin looking for other opportunities to point out the exception to any rule anybody can state. They delight in cross-examination of the unsuspecting, just looking for somebody's bubble of idealism floating around so they can pop it with their shiny new pin of skeptical analysis. When they do that, they fail to realize that when some of those bubbles pop, out goes much of the feeling of trust, loyalty, harmony, and sincerity so essential to preserving the Spirit of the Lord.

If that begins to happen in *our* ward, in *our* home, or in *our* marriage, we may be eroding the fragile fabric of trust that binds us together in all loving relationships. People may come away from their encounters with us wondering how we can possibly have a deep commitment to the gospel and say some of the things we say.

I am not saying we should always just smile and nod our approval, implying that everything is wonderful and that our highest hope is for everybody to have a nice day. That is level one. I *am* suggesting that we must realize the potential for harm as well as good that can come with what education and experience can do to our minds and our way of dealing with other people.

These dangers are not limited to our relations with others. They can become very personal, prying into our own hearts in unhealthy ways. The ability to acknowledge ambiguity is not a final form of enlightenment. Once our increased tolerance and patience enable us to look longer and harder at difficult questions and pat answers, we must be very careful, lest our basic stance toward spiritual things gradually shift from committed to noncommittal. That is not a healthy posture.

Indeed, in many ways, a Church member who moves from a stage of commitment to a stage of being tentative and noncommittal is in a worse position than one who has never experienced a basic commitment.

The previously committed person may too easily assume he has already been through the positive mental attitude routine and knows better now, as he judges things. He may assume that being submissive, meek, obedient, and humble is the "been there, done that" part of his life and he has now outgrown the need to be that way again. Those are the assumptions of a hardened heart.

I once had an experience that taught me a great lesson about the way a highly developed tolerance for being realistic can inhibit the workings of the Spirit in our lives. When I had been on my mission in Germany about a year, I was assigned to work with a brand-new missionary named Elder Keeler, who had just arrived fresh from converting, so he thought, all the flight attendants on the plane from New York to Frankfurt. Within a few days of his arrival, I was called to a meeting in another city and left him to work in our city with another new missionary whose companion went with me. I returned late that night.

The next morning I asked how his day had gone. His face broke into an enthusiastic smile, and he said they had found a family who would surely join the Church. In our mission, it was rare to see anyone join the Church, let alone a whole family. I asked for more details, but in his excitement he had forgotten to write down either the family's name or their address. All he could remember was that they lived on the top floor of a five-story apartment house, and he thought he'd recognize the name posted next to the doorbell if we just walked through enough apartment houses.

"MANTINI" DISEASE STRIKES AGAIN."

Great, I thought to myself as I contemplated all those flights of stairs. He also explained that he knew so little German that he had exchanged only a few words with the woman who answered the door. But he did think she wanted us to come back, and he wanted us to go find her so I could talk to her that very minute. I explained that the people who don't slam the door in our faces do not necessarily intend to join the Church, but off we went, mostly to humor him. He couldn't remember the street name, either, so we picked a likely spot in our tracting area and began climbing up and down those endless polished staircases.

After a frustrating hour, I decided I had to level with him. Based on my many months of experience, I said it simply wasn't worth our time to try any longer. I had developed a tolerance for the realities of missionary work in Europe and simply knew more than he did about it. His eyes filled with tears and his lower lip began to tremble. "Elder Hafen," he said, "I came on my mission to find the honest in heart. The Spirit *told* me that that woman will someday be a member of the Church."

I mumbled something like, "Maybe the Spirit was telling you to write down the name and address."

Then I decided to teach him a lesson. So I raced him up one staircase after another until I thought he'd be ready to drop. "Elder Keeler," I asked, "had enough?"

"No," he said. "We've got to find her."

I began to smolder. I stepped up the pace and decided to move so fast he would beg to stop. Maybe then he would get the message.

Finally, out of breath at the top of one more long staircase, we found the apartment. "I think that's the name!" he said. A woman answered the door. He jabbed my ribs with his elbow and whispered, "That's her, Elder. That's the one! Talk to her!"

Not long ago, Marie and I were with that woman, her husband, and all of their four children and their spouses in the Frankfurt Germany Temple. We watched in humility and gratitude as her husband, now an authorized temple sealer, performed the eternal sealing for their youngest daughter and her husband. The mother has been a Relief Society president. The father has been a bishop. Three of their children have served missions, and all four have been sealed in temple marriages to other faithful European Latter-day Saints. Despite whatever ambiguities of their own they may yet need to face, they are raising the next generation of their posterity in the full light of the gospel.

That experience is a lesson I can never forget about the limitations of skepticism and the tolerance for ambiguity that comes with learning and experience. I hope that I will never be so aware of "reality" that I am unresponsive to heavenly whisperings.

The most productive response to ambiguity is at level three, where we see things not only with our eyes wide open but with our hearts wide open as well. When we do that, there will be many times when we are called upon to take action, even though we need more evidence before knowing exactly what to do. Such occasions may range from following the counsel of the prophets when we don't understand the reason behind their counsel to accepting a Church calling when we are too busy to take on any more duties. My experience has taught me always to give the Lord and His Church the benefit of any doubts I may have when such a case seems too close to call.

CHOICE POINT

The willingness to be believing and accepting in these cases is a very different matter from blind obedience. It is, rather, a loving and knowing kind of obedience.

The English writer G. K. Chesterton once distinguished among optimists, pessimists, and improvers, which roughly correspond to the three levels we've discussed about dealing with ambiguity. He concluded that both the optimists and the pessimists look too much at only one side of things. Neither the extreme optimists nor the extreme pessimists will ever be of much help in *improving* human conditions, because people can't solve problems unless they are willing to acknowledge that a problem exists while also retaining enough genuine loyalty to do something about it.

Chesterton observed that the evil of the excessive optimist (level one) is that he will "defend the indefensible. He is the jingo of the universe; he will say, 'My cosmos, right or wrong.' He will be less inclined to the reform of things; more inclined to a sort of front-bench official answer to all attacks, soothing every one with assurances. He will not wash the world, but whitewash the world."[1]

On the other hand, the evil of the pessimist (level two) is "not that he chastises gods and men, but that he does not love what he chastises."

In being the so-called "candid friend," said Chesterton, the pessimist is not really candid. "He is keeping something back—his own gloomy pleasure in saying unpleasant things. He has a secret desire to hurt, not merely to help. . . . [H]e is using the ugly knowledge which was allowed him [in order] to strengthen the army, to discourage people from joining it."[2]

In going on to describe the improvers (level three), Chesterton illustrated by referring to women who tend to be loyal to those who need them: "Some stupid people started the idea that because women obviously back up their own people through everything, therefore women are blind and do not see anything. They can hardly have known any women. The same women who are ready to defend their men through thick and thin . . . are almost morbidly lucid about the thinness of his excuses or the thickness of his head. . . . Love is not blind; that is the last thing it is. Love is bound; and the more it is bound the less it is blind."[3]

Chesterton's arranging of these categories makes me think of one other way to compare the differing perspectives people bring to the way they cope with ambiguity. Consider the metaphorical image of the hymn "Lead, Kindly Light." At level one, people either do not or cannot see that there are *both* a kindly light and an encircling gloom; or even if they see both, they don't see the difference between the light and the gloom. At level two, the difference is acutely apparent, but one's acceptance of the ambiguity might be so completely pessimistic as to say, "Remember that the hour is darkest just before everything goes totally black."

We best understand how the kindly light can lead us when we are at level three, with both our eyes and our hearts wide open:

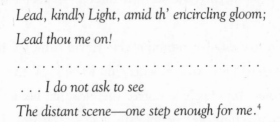

> *Lead, kindly Light, amid th' encircling gloom;*
> *Lead thou me on!*
>
> . . . .
>
> *. . . I do not ask to see*
> *The distant scene—one step enough for me.*[4]

I offer a final illustration of someone who stood at level three. He understood level two, because his eyes were fully open to the reality, including some of the pain, of seeing things for what they were. Yet he had moved beyond that to a third level where his mature perspective permitted him to subordinate what he saw with those wide-open eyes to what he felt in his wide-open heart.

The man in this case was my father, who died some years ago. At the time of this incident, he was in his mid-fifties and very involved in a busy professional life, with heavy obligations that often took him out of town for several days at a time. He was tired. At a much earlier time in his life he had served for ten years in a stake presidency and had fulfilled numerous other Church assignments.

One day a good friend approached him to say that he had just been called to be the bishop of their ward. He felt he couldn't possibly accept the assignment unless my father would serve as his first counselor.

It is one thing to be called as a bishop's counselor when one is young and full of enthusiasm and one's time is not heavily committed. One might understandably have a different attitude at a later, busier time in life. Here are the inner thoughts of my father's heart as he wrote them that day in his journal:

"My first reaction was, if it be possible, let this cup pass from me. . . . I know something of the work required of a bishopric; it is a constant, continual grind; there is no let up. . . . I am busy and my state affairs demand what spare time and energy I have. In some respects I am not humble and prayerful enough; I have not always been willing to submit unquestioningly to all the decisions of the Church . . . but neither do I feel that I can say no to any call that is made by the Church, and so now I add to my first reaction, 'Nevertheless, not as I will, but as Thou wilt.'

"I will resolve to do it as best I can. There will be times when I will chafe under the endless meetings, but I am going to get in tune with the program of the Church in every way. I do not intend to get sanctimonious, but I know there must be no reservations in my heart about my duties and responsibilities. The work of the Church will have to come first. It will not be hard for me to pay my tithing and attend regularly, as I have been doing that. But . . . I will have to get to the temple more often. . . . I will have to become better acquainted with the ward members and be genuinely interested in them and their problems. . . . I will have to learn to love every one of them and to dispose myself in such a way that they might find it possible to feel the same toward me. Perhaps in my weak way I will have to try and live as close to the Lord as we expect the General Authorities to do."

Perhaps my appreciation for understatement and my personal knowledge that my father was an honest man make that statement seem to me a more striking example of dealing humbly with ambiguity than it really is. But his statement stirs me to want to be as childlike as my education has taught me to be tough minded.

I hope we might be honest and courageous enough to face squarely the uncertainties we encounter, try to understand them, and then do something about them. Perhaps then we will not be living on borrowed light. "Love is not blind; that is the last thing it is. Love is bound; and the more it is bound, the less it is blind."

Part IV

FAITH, REASON, AND SPIRITUAL GROWTH

Chapter 7

HEBREWS AND GREEKS

In exploring now the relationship between the life of the spirit and the life of the mind, I refer to the example of Elder Neal A. Maxwell as a mentoring model.[1] Elder Maxwell showed us not only how to balance the natural tensions between faith and reason but also how to move beyond those tensions to a higher level of resolution.

When he first invited me to work on his biography in 1999, I believed that the main theme of his life story would be his contribution to the Church as a role model for educated Latter-day Saints, showing how religious faith and intellectual rigor are mutually reinforcing. Through both his public and his private ministries, he had been a great mentor on such issues for thousands of students, teachers, and other Church members.

However, my research on his life revealed a different core message from the one I had expected to find. Personal Christian discipleship is really the central message of Elder Maxwell's life and teachings. His background and contributions as an educator and scholar still matter a great deal; in fact, they matter even more when we also know that his life story is a kind of guidebook on seeking to be a true follower of Christ.

In my own life (and I'm only one among many others), his mentoring about reason and faith prepared me to benefit even more from his later, higher-level mentoring on spiritual questions about being and becoming. To talk about these ascending phases of his influence, I must go back to my student days at Brigham Young University in 1963.

The first semester after my mission to Germany, I enrolled in a small Honors religion class called "Your Religious Problems." The teacher was West Belnap, the dean of religion at BYU. The format for each class hour consisted primarily of a student presentation. The student would identify a religious problem, research the issues, and then lead a class discussion on the topic. The other students then wrote their thoughts about the problem and submitted them to our teacher and to that day's presenter.

The first time I ever noticed Marie Kartchner from Bountiful was in that class when she presented her religious problem: "How can I bring the influence of the Holy Ghost more into my life?" Almost every class day, a small group of us, including Marie, would keep talking after class, out into the hallway and across the campus. Coming to know Marie in that way actually solved my biggest religious problem, when that friendship blossomed into our marriage. In the past forty-plus years, those same lively gospel conversations have continued on, with Marie's intuitive insights always enriching my mind and heart, making me want to live better.

The problem I presented to our class was something like this: "How much should we develop our minds and think for ourselves, and how much should we rely on Church authority and spiritual guidance?" These were honest questions for me. I was experiencing what Catholic sociologist Thomas O'Dea had described in 1957 as "Mormonism's most significant problem." He thought the Church's "great emphasis on [higher] education" created an inevitable conflict for young Latter-day Saints, because he believed the Church's literalistic and authoritarian approach to religion would collide with the skepticism and personal independence fostered by university studies. Toward the end of his book *The Mormons*, O'Dea wrote, "The encounter of Mormonism and modern secular learning is one that is still taking place. . . . Upon [the] outcome [of this source of strain and conflict] will depend . . . the future of Mormonism."[2]

I could see from BYU's very existence that the Church was deeply committed to higher education, and I had returned from my mission in Europe with a high awareness of my own limited education, which fueled my hunger to learn. I was close to some faithful Latter-day Saint university teachers whose examples helped motivate that desire. One of them liked to remind me that Elder J. Golden Kimball had said we can't expect the Holy Ghost to do our thinking for us. Another had a great love for literature and the arts, and he emphasized that students needed both discipline and personal creativity to develop their God-given gifts.

One influential teacher from that era recently passed away in Provo—Reid Nibley, Hugh Nibley's younger brother. Reid was a consummate artist at the piano. He was the Utah Symphony's official pianist and taught for years on the BYU music faculty. He also wrote the words and music to the Primary song, "I Know My Father Lives."[3] He was my piano teacher in my mid-teens. I lived in St. George and went to Salt Lake City to study with him during the summer. He deeply affected my life, opening my eyes not only about the meaning of real musical skill but to a much larger world of thought and perspective than the one I had known in my small home town.

Reid Nibley loved the Lord with depth and meekness. Sometimes he would tell me that a heightened sensitivity to music would increase my sensitivity to spiritual things. I can still see him sitting cross-legged on a chair near the piano bench, quoting from Doctrine and Covenants 59 in his animated, optimistic voice that the Lord had given us nature and the arts "for the benefit and the use of man, both to please the eye and to gladden the heart; . . . to strengthen the body and to enliven the soul" (vv. 18–19). When I was about sixteen, someone asked me to list my heroes. I listed only two—Vic Wertz, who played right field for the Detroit Tigers baseball team, and Reid Nibley.

Later I had a mission president whom I also loved, but he saw the world very differently from the way these teachers did. He introduced me to precious doctrines about knowing the Lord and relying on the

Spirit. I came to prize those doctrines when I saw their fruits in our missionary work. He liked to quote Proverbs: "Trust in the Lord with all thine heart; and lean not unto thine own understanding" (Proverbs 3:5). He would cite the Gospel of John, emphasizing Christ's total reliance on the Father: "I speak not of myself: but the Father that dwelleth in me, he doeth the works" (John 14:10). He often said, "Christ was the most unoriginal man who ever lived. He did only what the Father told him to do." He also once warned us to stay away from people who took literature and the arts too seriously. Once he said, "Don't think too much."

Then, just after my mission and before I went to BYU, I spent some time with a seminary teacher whom I greatly admired. When he asked what I planned to study, I said I wanted to learn everything I could about such subjects as history, literature, and philosophy. He replied with great concern that I should avoid those subjects, because they can easily lead people into what he called intellectual apostasy.

So the religious problem I presented to our class reflected the confusion I felt in trying to reconcile the conflicting viewpoints among these teachers. West Belnap's comment to me after my presentation was, "Well, some of our people have it in their heads, and others have it in their hearts. I think the best way is to have it in both places." I understood that as a call for balance.

Brother Belnap's counsel helped me decide to reject an either/or, "phase one" approach to my questions. This elementary phase seemed to require a permanent, categorical choice between religious conservatism and religious liberalism. But neither of those choices made sense to me, because I had seen problems with both extremes.

For example, I saw the ultraconservative extreme in phase one as overzealous and unchecked religiosity. I had a stake missionary companion who was sure the Holy Ghost would give him the answer for every detail of his life and thought. He was always writing in a little book the things he believed the Spirit was telling him. He would dust off his feet after we left the door of someone who didn't want to hear our message. Only a few years later, he felt God had called him to leave the Church and become the leader of an apostate group. His overzealousness eventually had a tragic ending—for him, his family, and his followers.

I was also called to work closely with two very different student-ward bishops, who leaned toward the opposite extremes in phase one—and who, together, illustrated the broad spectrum of personalities and attitudes within the Church. One of these bishops was very authoritarian and extremely distrustful of all academic disciplines. The other was unusually free-thinking and highly academic. He said he was close enough to several senior Church leaders that he was aware of certain leaders' personal flaws. That concern ate away at him, eventually compromising his willingness to follow counsel from these leaders. Some years later he too left the Church.

These experiences reinforced my inclination to seek what I'll call phase two: a balanced approach to the religiously liberal and religiously conservative tendencies I had seen. I felt that I didn't need to make a permanent choice between my heart and my head.

Some years later I had an opportunity to explore this concept further in a BYU class I was teaching. My summary to my students went something like this: The tension between faith and reason is a challenge with a very long history. During His mortal life, Christ taught His gospel almost exclusively to people of a Hebrew background. But not many years after His death, Gentiles from the Roman Empire who had a Greek heritage began entering the Church. Other factors increased their influence, until Christianity became the official religion of the Roman Empire in the fourth century. That huge historical shift merged the Hebrew and Greco-Roman cultures, combining two very different religious traditions.

As one historian put it, this merger superimposed the "entire Hebraic Tradition . . . upon Classical [Greek and Roman] culture."[4] And because Greek thought had by then so heavily influenced the Roman Empire, another historian could say, "Here were two races [the Greeks and the Hebrews], living not very far apart, yet for the most part in complete ignorance of each other. . . . It was the fusion of what was most characteristic in these two cultures—the religious earnestness of the Hebrews with the reason and humanity of the Greeks—which was to form the basis of later European culture."[5]

A few years ago I read a fine article by BYU's Daniel Peterson that shed light on the implications of this historical watershed. He wrote that the shift of Christianity's center of gravity from Jerusalem to the

Greek-speaking world gradually cut the New Testament's ties to its roots in the Hebraic world of the Old Testament. The resulting Greek influence preserved Christ's words in the New Testament only in the Greek language. "Mormons," wrote Brother Peterson, "recognize in this [Greek absorption of Christianity] at least one aspect of what they term 'the Great Apostasy.'"[6]

I told my students that the gospel contains strands that connect to both the Hebrew and the Greek elements in our heritage. That helped me see why I had found the conflicts I did in my student days.

Without attempting a complete comparison, let us consider an example that reflects a combining of both the Greek and the Hebrew traditions. Most United States coins bear two familiar mottoes: "Liberty" and "In God We Trust." The personal liberty of the individual was a key element in the hierarchy of Greek values. In the Greek heritage, man is the measure of all things. For Socrates, nothing was more important than to "know thyself," and the ultimate goal was to ennoble man through reason.

But the phrase on the other side of the coin comes from the Hebrew tradition—"In God We Trust." That idea spoke directly to the Hebrew soul, who did try to trust in the Lord with all his heart and lean not to his own understanding. The goal of the Hebrew pattern was to glorify God, not man; and one reached this goal through faith and obedience to divine authority, not by relying on human reasoning. In this example from the differing but overlapping Greek and Hebrew worlds we find the seeds of countless arguments about reason versus faith and individual liberty versus authority in our religious life.

The restored gospel exhibits elements from both traditions. For example, the gospel places high value on both personal liberty and reason. No other religion or philosophy takes a higher view of man's nature and individual potential. Consider these phrases: "This is my work and my glory—to bring to pass the immortality and eternal life of man" (Moses 1:39). "I am a child of God."[7] "Man was also in the beginning with God" (D&C 93:29).

Consider also the place of reason in our doctrine about testimony: "Study it out in your mind" (D&C 9:8). "All things [in nature] denote there is a God" (Alma 30:44). "The greatness of the evidences" for spiritual truth (Helaman 5:50).[8] And Elder John A. Widtsoe entitled his classic book on this subject *A Rational Theology*.

On the other hand, the gospel teaches that all blessings are predicated on obedience to God. Further, faith in God is not only the first principle of the gospel but an essential check against unrestrained liberty and reason. When the free individual chooses to disobey God, he not only rejects Divine authority but also damages his future liberty. As the Lord said, "Here is the agency of man, and here is the condemnation of man; because that which was from the beginning is plainly manifest unto them, and they receive not the light" (D&C 93:31).

Imagine two circles that partially overlap each other. One circle represents the Greek tradition, with reason and individualism as samples. The other circle represents the Hebrew tradition, with faith

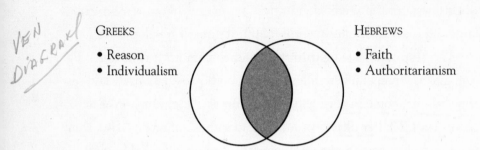

VEN DIAGRAM

GREEKS
- Reason
- Individualism

HEBREWS
- Faith
- Authoritarianism

and authoritarianism as samples. On the left end of the spectrum, outside the area of overlap, we see the Greek tradition alone. At the right end of the spectrum, also outside the overlap, is the Hebrew tradition alone. We will be in trouble if our individualistic Greek strain cuts us loose from the anchoring authoritarianism of our Hebrew strain. That's what happened with the former bishop I mentioned, who could not reason his way through the flaws he perceived in some Church leaders. His unchecked commitment to reason alone eventually took him out of the Church. We might consider those on the far left end of this spectrum as cultural Mormons, who accept only the part of the gospel that meets their standard of rationality.

At the other extreme, my former stake missionary companion exemplified the Hebrew strain gone wild. Unchecked by reason and common sense, he veered off the edge and became what we might call a cultist Mormon. In other words, we can go off the deep end at either side of the spectrum.

The area of overlap, where the individualistic and authoritarian principles coexist, is where we live most productively. Here authoritarianism acts as a check against unbridled individualism, and individualism acts as a check against unbridled authoritarianism. Both principles are true, and both play a role in our decisions and attitudes—though the outcome in particular cases may vary, depending on the circumstances. Similar check-and-balance interaction occurs between faith and reason, which are both within the area of overlap.

President Spencer W. Kimball once spoke to a BYU audience about our "double heritage" of secular knowledge and revealed truth. He said we must become "bilingual" in speaking the language of education and the language of the Spirit.[9]

Within the overlap area of our dual heritage, true principles drawn from the two traditions can sometimes compete and conflict. For example, the idea of "liberty" on our coins is in natural tension with the idea of "in God we trust." If we really trust in God, we must at times place limits on our own liberty. Christ's teachings are full of similar paradoxes—that is, true principles that seem to contradict each other but that can be reconciled by higher doctrines. Consider, for example, the principles of justice and mercy. At times they may seem to be in opposition, but both are essential in the higher doctrine of the Atonement.

Gospel teachings contain other paradoxes. For example, the Savior taught us to "let your light so shine before this people, that they may see your good works and glorify your Father who is in heaven" (3 Nephi 12:16). Yet elsewhere He taught, "Do not your alms before men to be seen of them" (3 Nephi 13:1; Matthew 6:1). In some circumstances Christ was called the "Prince of Peace" (Isaiah 9:6) and promised to give peace to His disciples (John 14:27). Yet elsewhere He said, "I came not to send peace, but a sword" (Matthew 10:34).

In presenting these ideas to my class, I concluded that Brother Belnap was right—it is best to nourish our religious commitments in both our hearts and our heads, even if doing so means we must sometimes work through seeming paradoxes. The process of reconciling competing true values requires effort, but it can yield very good fruit.

Then I told my students that the best way to resolve such tensions is not just through abstract discussion but also through following the personal examples of people whose lives represent balanced, productive resolutions. One role model I offered them was Elder Neal A. Maxwell, whose heart and head worked so well together. For example, he once said to the faculty at BYU, "We cannot let the world condemn our value system by calling attention to our professional mediocrity."[10]

He also told BYU students and faculty to be unafraid of dealing with the world outside the Church, because they are needed there. They must be like Joseph of Egypt, he said. In today's famine of the spirit, they should lean into the fray and draw on divine powers in their professional work, so they are part of society's solutions—not just another hungry mouth to feed. He also told LDS teachers that they should take both scholarship and discipleship seriously, because consecrated scholarship brings together both the life of the mind and the life of the spirit.[11]

Elder Maxwell had first developed these attitudes during his own days as a university student, when he instinctively looked for ways to integrate secular and religious knowledge. Even as a young political science major, he didn't think the field of political theory was complete without including the gospel's teachings about government and about man's nature. As his experience grew, so did his confidence that the findings of the academic disciplines would never seriously challenge gospel teachings. For him, every dimension of the gospel was relevant to modern social problems and, whenever possible, he thought LDS scholars should take their research premises from gospel teachings.

Elder Maxwell drew on these attitudes when he actively encouraged LDS scholars to do the kind of work now being done at BYU's Maxwell Institute. To him, the internal evidence for the Book of Mormon's legitimacy was so strong that it was simply unscientific to think the book was concocted in the nineteenth century.

He often reminded LDS scholars that he wasn't interested in trying to prove in some scientific way that the Book of Mormon is true—a task that, like proving the existence or nonexistence of God, is simply beyond the realm of what science is able to do. Rather, he saw faithful scholarship as a source of defense, not offense. That kind of scholarship has the modest but crucial purpose of nourishing a climate in which voluntary belief is free to take root and grow. Only when belief is not compelled, by external evidence or otherwise, can it produce the growth that is the promised fruit of faith.

Chapter 8

THE THINGS OF ETERNITY

I return now to my own autobiographical journey because as I grew older, I kept having experiences that pushed me beyond that second phase of balance toward a third phase of meaning. For example, I remember talking with a Latter-day Saint college teacher who described his religious convictions as "an intelligent faith." As an example of a phase two response, his attitude seemed balanced and constructive. But as I reflected more on his language, something felt amiss—not about him personally but about modifying the word *faith* with a word like *intelligent*. I remembered how President Marion G. Romney had answered the missionary who asked, "Why don't we baptize more intelligent people?"

President Romney quoted Doctrine and Covenants 93:36–37: "The glory of God is intelligence, or, in other words, light and truth. Light and truth forsake that evil one." Then he said to the missionary, "A converted person forsakes evil and embraces light and truth. So what kind of person is he?"

After a pause, the surprised missionary said, "An intelligent one?"
President Romney said, "That's right."

About this same time, a close friend my age was declining physically from multiple sclerosis. I had seen him gradually lose his ability to walk, to stand, and then to sit. During the stage when he was fully bedridden, his wife passed away from cancer. His family wheeled him into her funeral on a mobile bed.

Not long after his wife's funeral, my friend and I had a visit in his home. The more he talked, the more amazed I was at the spirit of peace and light that surrounded him. He said he couldn't stop thinking about how fortunate his life had been—so blessed by the woman he'd married, by the children the Lord had given them, by their rich life together in their wholesome little town. He chuckled as he said how glad he was now that he and his wife took so many "happily ever after" trips in their early years, even though they had a hard time affording it.

And he kept talking about his admiration for the pioneers, the ones who left Nauvoo and helped settle the town where he lived. He felt so thankful to them. He'd been thinking about why they needed the temple endowment before leaving Nauvoo for the wilderness. Every word and feeling that came from him was genuine. There was no trace of self-pity. The light in his face and the spirit in the room told me that I was watching the sacred process of sanctification, which his deteriorating physical condition paradoxically seemed to enhance.

That night I felt drawn to read in Doctrine and Covenants 101:2–5: "I, the Lord, have suffered the affliction to come upon them . . . ; yet I will own them, and they shall be mine in that day when I shall come to make up my jewels. Therefore, they must needs be chastened and tried, even as Abraham, who was commanded to offer up his only son. For all those who will not endure chastening, but deny me, *cannot* be sanctified" (emphasis added). Is it possible that our sanctification and acceptance by the Lord cannot take place without affliction, chastening, and sacrifice?

Soon after this experience, I had similar feelings as I watched our son Tom and his wife, Tracy, experience the birth of a child with severe cerebral palsy. Because this baby had threatened to come too early, Tracy had been on total bed rest for nine weeks. Despite bedsores and increasing medical threats, she became very single-minded about hanging on to that baby until it could survive outside the womb. One night Tracy sensed something about how her determination and her sacrifice were allowing her to emulate the Savior's example—giving up her body's strength to strengthen her baby's body. That night she said to Tom, "I am realizing that giving this baby my strength is not a burden. It is a privilege."

After being born, the baby was confined to the hospital for ten more weeks before coming home to a life in which she would never walk, nor talk, nor feed herself. She is now twelve, and what a child of light she is! Her name is Chaya, which in Hebrew means "life."

Soon after Chaya's birth, Tom gave her a blessing, during which he realized that this was a defining moment in his own life. He sensed that all he and Tracy had done and learned up to that point wasn't very important by comparison. What mattered now was their awareness that God knew their circumstances and that this child's condition was not accidental nor arbitrary; in fact, there was great purpose in it. They felt that they were both being asked to offer the sacrifice of a broken heart and contrite spirit, which was somehow making the Lord's own sacrifice more personally accessible to them.

Something about these two experiences set me to thinking about that summary on the Greeks and Hebrews I had shown my students— and about that college teacher's comments on an "intelligent faith." The experiences with my friend and my granddaughter defied rational explanation, and yet I had witnessed the sanctifying effects of those afflictions. I sensed that a balanced quest for knowledge, as valuable as that is, cannot be our ultimate end. Simply *knowing* something will not sanctify us, will not make us capable of being in God's presence. And the circumstances that sanctify us often won't be rational ones. By its very nature, faith ultimately takes us beyond the boundaries of reason. Thus someone who conditions his faith on its being rationally intelligent may shrink from a sanctifying experience—and therefore not discover what the experience could teach.

At the same time, even if yielding to such transforming experiences is necessarily a leap of faith, we can't go there until we've walked as far as the light of our search for knowledge allows. And a lifetime of trying to make sense of mortality (especially on days when we wonder if it is really making sense) gives us the experience we must eventually have to appreciate the meaning of our sanctification after it has been completed.

In phase two, we prize the value of individualism and reason, and we also prize the value of God's authority and our faith in Him. We would not return to a simplistic phase one that completely excludes either reason or faith.

But phase three invites us to realize that a balanced approach alone won't be enough when we encounter the most demanding experiences of our spiritual growth. When we find ourselves stretched to our extremity we must stand on a new level that lets us draw more deeply on our Hebrew roots than our Greek roots.

No wonder Elder Neal A. Maxwell said we must always have our citizenship in Jerusalem and use our passports to go to Athens.[1] In fact, part of the sacrifice the Lord may require is that we accept what He may "inflict" upon us (Mosiah 3:19) without understanding to our rational satisfaction why we should be lost in some dark night of the soul. Eventually the light of Christ's atoning power can pierce our darkness and bless us with understanding, but we may receive no such witness until after the trial of our faith (Ether 12:6).

Even with his admiration for fine scholarship, Elder Maxwell believed that the life of a disciple-scholar is more about consecration than it is about scholarship. To be sure, he believed that "academic scholarship [can be] a form of worship . . . another dimension of consecration." But he also said, "Genius without meekness is not enough to qualify for discipleship." On one occasion, he concluded: "Though I have spoken of the disciple-scholar, in the end all the hyphenated words come off. We are finally [just] disciples—men and women of Christ."[2]

He once told me that he felt sorry for those who overdo the scholarly part of trying to be disciple-scholars. They tend to measure the gospel and the Church by what they have learned in their academic disciplines rather than the other way around. For that reason, he said, they can ironically become anti-intellectual about the gospel—not seeing its depth, its applications, its beauty, and its fruits, which go far beyond merely being active in the Church.

As part of his own discipleship, Elder Maxwell consciously cultivated the qualities of meekness and submissiveness—precisely because he knew all about pride's subtle seductions. Even the Greeks had no use for hubris. Elder Maxwell had seen very accomplished people become too impressed with themselves—the learned who "think they are wise" and therefore "hearken not unto the counsel of God," for they suppose "they know of themselves" (2 Nephi 9:28). Those who are, as Jacob said, "puffed up because of their learning, and their wisdom" suffer the great loss that the "happiness which is prepared for the saints" "shall be hid from them" (2 Nephi 9:42–43).

C. S. Lewis once wrote, "I reject at once [the] idea that . . . scholars and poets [are] intrinsically more pleasing to God than scavengers and bootblacks. . . . The work of a Beethoven and the work of a charwoman become spiritual on precisely the same condition, that of being [humbly] offered to God. . . . This does not mean that it is for anyone a mere toss-up whether he should sweep rooms or compose symphonies. A mole must dig to the glory of God and a cock must crow." But if one's circumstances give him a "learned life," said Lewis, let him lead "that life to the glory of God."

In living a learned life, Lewis noted that personal humility is essential; otherwise, we may "come to love knowledge—*our* knowing—more than the thing known: to delight not in the exercise of our talents but in the fact that they are ours, or even in the reputation they bring us. Every success in the scholar's life increases this danger. If it becomes irresistible, he must give up his scholarly work."

Still, continued Lewis, "the learned life [is] especially important today. If all the world were Christian, it might not matter if all the world were uneducated. . . . To be ignorant and simple now—not to be able to meet the enemies on their own ground—would be to throw down our weapons, and to betray our uneducated brethren who have, under God, no defense but us against the intellectual attacks of the heathen. Good philosophy must exist, if for no other reason, [than] because bad philosophy needs to be answered."[3]

Studying Elder Maxwell's life showed me that even though he was an ideal role model for educated Latter-day Saints, his life's primary message was more about becoming a true, disciplined follower of Christ than about learning and scholarship.

As a young man, he was incredibly attentive to developing the skills of self-discipline and self-improvement. One sees the same determined effort in his approach to playing basketball, raising prize pigs in a 4-H project, learning to write in high school, serving in combat during World War II, studying government as a college student and as

a staffer in the United States Senate, finding a better way to do missionary work in Canada, or studying leadership in the Church.

One friend who first saw Neal's fierce tenacity during his years as
an administrator at the University of Utah said that he "tried very, very
hard over the years to make himself a better person. For most people,
New Year's resolutions don't last. But his do." Another lifelong friend
said, "No one I know requires such extreme effort of himself."

I mention this general commitment to self-mastery to put Elder
Maxwell's quest for discipleship into context. He always had a believing heart and a desire to serve the Lord. But during his adult years, his
understanding of the word *disciple* developed significantly—and delib-
erately. He first used the written word *disciple* in the 1960s as a syn-
onym for "Church member." Then during his years as Commissioner
of Church Education in the early 1970s, he became concerned about
the growing influence of modern secularism. He began using *disciples*
to describe those Church members who resist secular siren calls.
Within a few years, he had grown close to several Church members
who were coping with adversity in ways that enhanced their spiritual
growth. He soon felt that these people were the real disciples.

His call to the Twelve in 1981 turned his full attention to becoming a more faithful disciple of Christ himself. Reflecting his great determination to live better, his writing and his talks now focused more on
the disciple's personal relationship with Christ and how the Lord will
help true disciples learn such Christlike attributes as patience, hope,
and lowliness of heart.

He also began to see discipleship more as a process than a single choice, and he realized that adversity is sometimes a tool the Lord uses to teach His followers the attributes they need for their development. That is why he wrote, in terms that would one day take on such personal meaning for him, that "the very act of choosing to be a disciple . . . can bring to us a certain special suffering. . . . [Such] suffering and chastening . . . is the . . . dimension that comes with deep discipleship," when the Lord takes us "to the very edge of our faith; we teeter at the edge of our trust . . . [in] a form of learning as it is administered at the hands of a loving Father."[4]

No wonder, then, that in 1997 when he found he had an aggressive form of leukemia, he said, "I should have seen it coming." What did he mean? Neal Maxwell, the ardent student of discipleship, had signed up years earlier for divine tutoring, and his Tutor was now ready to teach him a course in personal and clinical graduate studies.

In his remaining seven years, he embraced the heart-wrenching process of sanctification as his final tutorial. Most people who experience a terminal illness can't help being consumed with their own suffering, but not Neal Maxwell. He saw himself as being in a time for testing and refining. And because he was not imprisoned by his own misery, he was free to reflect on what his new understanding could teach him and how it could help him teach others.

As a result, those who had known him for years now saw a new mellowness, greater empathy, increased spiritual sensitivity, and keener compassion for other people's needs. Elder Maxwell viewed this experience as a gift, not as an achievement. He knew the Lord was giving him a new, sanctified heart filled with divine attributes, and he said, "The natural man['s] . . . heart . . . is pretty self-centered and hard." But "adversity can squeeze out of us the [remaining] hypocrisy that's there. [So, for me,] it's been a great spiritual adventure, one I would not want to have missed. And even though this has [had high costs], it's been a great blessing."[5]

It is hard to describe how watching Elder Maxwell's experience, like watching the experience of my friend with multiple sclerosis, has changed my perspective about what I called my "religious problem." Those who taste sanctification must often pay such a terribly high price. How can they possibly understand the need for their suffering? Rather than looking for a rational explanation, Elder Maxwell would just quote Nephi: "I know that [God] loveth his children; nevertheless, I do not know the meaning of all things" (1 Nephi 11:17).

At about this point in my writing of this chapter, a visitor came to our home—a student at Brigham Young University whose parents Marie and I had met in another city a few months earlier. We had met them at a hospital, where his father was in the last stages of a terminal illness. Despite his tears and his questions, this father was exceptionally full of peace and purpose. He told us he knew his days were numbered, but he had accepted his stake president's challenge to read the scriptures with a true hunger to understand and internalize the doctrine of sanctification. His countenance, his manner, and his thoughts were very similar to what I had seen before—with my friend and with

Elder Maxwell. We offered words intended to give support and love, but he is the one who gave us spiritual perspective.

His son had stopped by to tell us that his father had passed away a few weeks before. Then he said he had learned about sanctification from his father during his final weeks, and that experience had permanently changed his view of life, including his daily priorities. Applying his father's perspective to his own life as a young man, he said he didn't want to wait until he had cancer; rather, he wanted to live in a different and better way *now*, closer to what he called "the things of eternity."

This student's visit somehow illustrated phase three for me, even though I still don't quite have the words to define that phase in my own development. I will leave you with the invitation to find your own words, but I will try at least to offer a picture of what I think phase three looks like. It is something about how the consecrated sacrifice of a broken heart and a contrite spirit blesses us with inner sight in our lives, including our religious questions. This perspective takes us to a higher spiritual realm than mere balance can ever lift us—even though standing on that balanced foundation helps us reach upward. This phase does not ask us to give up anything of value in our reasoning or in our own mental exertion, though it does recognize reason's limits. Indeed, from this vantage point, we need even more rigorous research and deeper inquiry, especially about protecting and nurturing the things of eternity.

Phase three also tells us that being a disciple-scholar is not so much about what we do or how we think but about who and what we are—and are becoming. In the course of Elder Maxwell's adult life, he gradually shifted his emphasis from large-scale macro concerns about secularization and social problems to the more focused, personal, micro concerns of how to live our lives. Not that the macro problems don't matter; he just knew that the micro problems are the ones we can do the most about. And in the long run, he knew that the gospel's way of changing the individual is the only lasting way to change society.

Remembering this about Elder Maxwell reminds me of one writer's comments from an essay on C. S. Lewis: "The kind of people we are is more important than what we can do to improve the world; indeed, being the kind of people we should and can be is the best, and sometimes the only, way to improve the world."[6]

So Elder Maxwell was right, both in what he said and in how he lived. In the end, there are no hyphenated words such as disciple-scholar. And if we are not true disciples, it won't matter much what kind of scholars we've been.

Swiss artist Eugene Burnand's painting of the Apostles John and Peter is the visual version of phase three. It is a picture worth more than a thousand words. The painting depicts John and Peter, true disciples, running to the tomb very early on the first Easter morning. In John's words, "they *ran* both together" until they reached the sepulcher (John 20:4; emphasis added).

The look on their faces, their eagerness and their energy, make me want to join them as they run to find Him. Watching them makes me want to ask them, and to ask myself, the Lord's question to Mary near the garden tomb that same day: "Whom seekest thou?" (John 20:15).

Eugene Burnand, *The Disciples Peter and John Running to the Sepulchre on the Morning of the Resurrection*, c. 1898

Marie first showed me how the faces of these two Apostles capture the ultimate tension between faith and reason. Since no one had ever risen from the dead before, it was completely irrational for John and Peter to expect that Christ would live again. No wonder they hadn't understood Him when He had said He must soon leave them: "a little while, and ye shall see me" and "your sorrow shall be turned into joy" (John 16:16, 20).

But their faces also show their faith and hope rising to overcome their rational doubts. And when John and Peter eventually did meet the risen Lord, their being faithful enough to see Him was the ultimate resolution of the tension they had felt between faith and reason. He is the ultimate resolution to everything.

Something about this painting speaks to me about taking action—moving, and moving now—early, as in the early morning and on the earliest Easter. We don't need to wait until we have a terminal disease to get serious about the things of eternity. May we feel *now* the excitement of quickening our step and arriving early as we run to meet Him. Whether as a student, a mother, a father, a scholar, a carpenter, or a secretary, may we work with all our hearts, and all of our minds, and to the glory of God. And may we hasten our desire to live closer to those eternal things and that eternal Presence, thus allowing the Lord to prepare us sooner and better for whatever further sanctifying tests may still await us.

NOTES

INTRODUCTION

1. Thomas S. Monson, "How Firm a Foundation," *Ensign*, November 2006, 62.
2. John Bartlett, *Familiar Quotations*, ed. Emily Morison Beck, 14th ed. (Boston: Little, Brown, 1968), 597.
3. Aldous Huxley, *Brave New World* (New York: HarperPerennial, 1969), chap. 17.

PART I. A DISCIPLE'S JOURNEY

CHAPTER 1. FROM DARKNESS TOWARD THE LIGHT

1. "Who's on the Lord's Side?" *Hymns of The Church of Jesus Christ of Latter-day Saints* (Salt Lake City: The Church of Jesus Christ of Latter-day Saints, 1985), no. 260.
2. "Be Still, My Soul," *Hymns*, no. 124; emphasis added.
3. "I'm Trying to Be like Jesus," *Children's Songbook* (Salt Lake City: The Church of Jesus Christ of Latter-day Saints, 1989), 78.
4. Jan Shipps, *Sojourner in the Promised Land: Forty Years among the Mormons* (Chicago: University of Illinois Press, 2000), 112.
5. Noah Feldman, "What Is It about Mormonism?" *New York Times Magazine*, 6 January 2008, 37.
6. Stopford A. Brooke, *The Poetry of Robert Browning* (New York: Thomas Y. Crowell, 1902), 136.
7. Bruce C. Hafen, *A Disciple's Life: The Biography of Neal A. Maxwell* (Salt Lake City: Deseret Book, 2002), 108–9.
8. Sheri L. Dew, *Go Forward with Faith: The Biography of Gordon B. Hinckley* (Salt Lake City: Deseret Book, 1996), 64.

9. Quoted in Marjorie Newton, *Southern Cross Saints: The Mormons in Australia* (Laie, Hawaii: Brigham Young University-Hawaii, Institute for Polynesian Studies, 1991), 158; capitalization standardized.

10. "There Is Sunshine in My Soul Today," *Hymns*, no. 227.

11. "God Rest Ye Merry, Gentlemen."

CHAPTER 2. "WITH YOU"—IN THE LIGHT OF HIS LOVE

1. Neal A. Maxwell, "Swallowed Up in the Will of the Father," *Ensign*, November 1995, 24.

2. "I Feel My Savior's Love," *Children's Songbook* (Salt Lake City: The Church of Jesus Christ of Latter-day Saints, 1989), 74.

3. Quoted in Donald L. Staheli, "Obedience—Life's Great Challenge," *Ensign*, May 1998, 82.

4. Author's notes of remarks in General Authority training meeting, April 2004.

5. Orval Hafen, journal, 1936; unpublished manuscript in author's possession.

6. Edward L. Kimball and Andrew E. Kimball Jr., *Spencer W. Kimball* (Salt Lake City: Bookcraft, 1977), 19.

7. Ibid., 20.

8. Ibid.

9. Ibid., 31.

10. Ibid.

11. L. A. Fleming, "The Settlements on the Muddy, 1865 to 1871: 'A Godforsaken Place,'" *Utah Historical Quarterly* 35 (1967): 147.

12. Conversation with Bill Cox, 6 October 2002.

13. Melvin S. Tagg, "The Life of Edward James Wood" (master's thesis, Brigham Young University, 1959), 10.

14. Joseph Smith, *Lectures on Faith* (Salt Lake City: Deseret Book, 1985), 6:7, 12.

15. Neal A. Maxwell, *A Time to Choose* (Salt Lake City: Deseret Book, 1972), 46.

16. Bruce C. Hafen, *A Disciple's Life: The Biography of Neal A. Maxwell* (Salt Lake City: Deseret Book, 2002), 20.

17. Harriet Beecher Stowe, "Still, Still with Thee," in *Masterpieces of Religious Verse*, ed. James Dalton Morrison (New York and London: Harper & Brothers, 1948), 75; emphasis added.

PART II. TESTIMONY

CHAPTER 3. HOW DO I KNOW?

1. Thomas S. Monson, "How Firm a Foundation," *Ensign*, November 2006, 62.

2. Brigham Young, *Journal of Discourses*, 26 vols. (London: Latter-day Saints' Book Depot, 1854-86), 1:20.

CHAPTER 4. REASON, FEELING, AND EXPERIENCE

1. Teachersdomain.org, Resource: Triangles and Arches in Architecture.
2. Joseph Smith, *Teachings of the Prophet Joseph Smith*, sel. Joseph Fielding Smith (Salt Lake City: Deseret Book, 1976), 151.
3. Francis S. Collins, *The Language of God: A Scientist Presents Evidence for Belief* (Free Press: New York, 2006), 2–3, 74.
4. Ibid., 30.
5. Carl Mosser and Paul Owen, "Mormon Scholarship, Apologetics, and Evangelical Neglect: Losing the Battle and Not Knowing It?" *Trinity Journal of Theology*, n.s. 19 (Fall 1998): 180–81, 179–80.
6. Neal A. Maxwell, *Plain and Precious Things* (Salt Lake City: Deseret Book, 1983), 4.
7. Austin Farrer, "Grete Clerk," in Jocelyn Gibb, comp., *Light on C. S. Lewis* (New York: Harcourt and Brace, 1965), 26, quoted in "Discipleship and Scholarship," *BYU Studies* 32, no. 3 (Summer 1992): 5.
8. Quoted in Arthur M. Abell, *Talks with Great Composers* (New York: Philosophical Library of New York, 1954), 5–6, 21, 64.
9. Leonard J. Arrington, *Brigham Young: American Moses* (New York: Alfred A. Knopf, 1985), 352, citing a Brigham Young family manuscript record of a talk for 28 November 1869.
10. "Count Your Blessings," *Hymns of The Church of Jesus Christ of Latter-day Saints* (Salt Lake City: The Church of Jesus Christ of Latter-day Saints, 1985), no. 241.

PART III. LOVE IS NOT BLIND

The two chapters in this part are a revised version of a chapter in Bruce C. Hafen, *The Believing Heart: Nourishing the Seed of Faith*, 2d ed. (Salt Lake City: Deseret Book, 1990).

CHAPTER 5. WHEN THINGS SEEM UNCERTAIN

1. Spencer W. Kimball, *Peter, My Brother*, Brigham Young University Speeches of the Year (Provo, Utah, 13 July 1971).
2. Orson F. Whitney, *Life of Heber C. Kimball* (Salt Lake City: Bookcraft, 1945), 450.

CHAPTER 6. BEYOND AMBIGUITY

1. G. K. Chesterton, *Orthodoxy* (Garden City, New York: Images Book, 1959), 69–70.
2. Ibid., 69.
3. Ibid., 71.
4. "Lead, Kindly Light," *Hymns of The Church of Jesus Christ of Latter-day Saints* (Salt Lake City: The Church of Jesus Christ of Latter-day Saints, 1985), no. 97.

PART IV. FAITH, REASON, AND SPIRITUAL GROWTH

CHAPTER 7. HEBREWS AND GREEKS

1. This chapter refers often to Elder Neal A. Maxwell because it is based on the annual Neal A. Maxwell Lecture given at Brigham Young University, Provo, Utah, 21 March 2008.
2. Thomas F. O'Dea, *The Mormons* (Chicago: University of Chicago Press, 1957), 240.
3. "I Know My Father Lives," *Children's Songbook* (Salt Lake City: The Church of Jesus Christ of Latter-day Saints, 1989), 5.
4. Rod William Horton and Vincent Foster Hopper, *Backgrounds of European Literature* (New York: Appleton-Century, 1954), 248.
5. H. D. F. Kitto, *The Greeks* (Baltimore: Penguin, 1969), 8.
6. Daniel C. Peterson, "Editor's Introduction: 'What Has Athens to Do with Jerusalem?' Apostasy and Restoration in the Big Picture," *FARMS Review of Books* 12, no. 2 (2000): xii.
7. "I Am a Child of God," *Children's Songbook* (Salt Lake City: The Church of Jesus Christ of Latter-day Saints, 1989), 2.
8. See pages 52–57 of this volume.
9. Spencer W. Kimball, "The Second Century of Brigham Young University," in *Speeches of the Year, 1975* (Provo: Brigham Young University Press, 1976), 244–45.
10. Quoted in Bruce C. Hafen, *A Disciple's Life: The Biography of Neal A. Maxwell* (Salt Lake City: Deseret Book, 2002), 380.
11. Ibid., 379–81.

CHAPTER 8. THE THINGS OF ETERNITY

1. Quoted in Bruce C. Hafen, *A Disciple's Life: The Biography of Neal A. Maxwell* (Salt Lake City: Deseret Book, 2002), 333.
2. Ibid., 379–80.
3. C. S. Lewis, *The Weight of Glory and Other Addresses* (New York: Macmillan, Collier Books, 1965), 26–28.
4. Hafen, *Disciple's Life*, 12.
5. Ibid., 558.
6. Richard John Neuhaus, "C. S. Lewis in the Public Square," *First Things* 88 (December 1998): 30.

INDEX